CUSTOM CAR
Modeling

Mark S. Gustavson

KALMBACH
BOOKS

Printed in the United States of America

99 00 01 02 03 04 05 06 07 08   10 9 8 7 6 5 4 3 2 1

Visit our website at
http://books.kalmbach.com
Secure online ordering available

Publisher's Cataloging in Publication
(Provided by Quality Books, Inc.)

Gustavson, Mark S.
   Custom car modeling / Mark S. Gustavson.
   — 1st ed.
   p. cm.
   ISBN 0-89024-342-5

   1. Automobiles—Models—Customizing.
I. Title

TL237.G87 1999   629.22´1
                                        QBI99-79

Book design: Lisa A. Zehner
Cover design: Kristi Ludwig
Cover photo: Jim Forbes

Acknowledgments

I want to acknowledge my indebtedness to some very close friends whose assistance has been instrumental in the creation of this book. First, much credit must go to Mike Barlow who has, for many years, tirelessly worked with me taking photographs for my articles in *Scale Auto Enthusiast* and *Car Modeler* magazines, including many that appear in this book (unless otherwise noted, all photos were taken by Mike Barlow). Second, I express gratitude to Bob Wick who not only penned the Foreword but extended his considerable editorial skills in reviewing the text. Third, my thanks go out to professional custom car painters George Layton and Rick Harris for their advice concerning Chapter Eight of this book. Fourth, my hearty thanks to Darryl Starbird—a childhood hero of mine—who allowed me to copy the photographs of his famous Predicta and Forcasta show cars for my personal files; one example of each can be seen here. Fifth, my appreciation is expressed to new friends Spencer Murray and Kurt McCormick, the creator and current owner/preservationist, respectively, of the famed Dream Truck, who not only created and preserved possibly the most recognized of all custom vehicles, but are deeply committed to the custom car hobby. They also have graciously permitted me to copy the entire photo library of the famous Truck, an example of which is displayed here. Last, I want to acknowledge the faithful help of Byron Bowman, owner of the famous Superior Paint Supply, who, for more than 20 years, has custom-mixed lacquer paints for me, often taking on nearly impossible assignments with good humor and sterling performance.

Contents

Dedication

In our hobby, as in every arena of human achievement, there are pivotal individuals who almost single-handedly change the complexion of an entire landscape. One such person was Bob Barnett. While not the first builder of scale replica custom vehicles, Bob was the most passionate and eloquent advocate of the replication of famous full-scale custom automobiles that the model car hobby has ever had. Pleasant and intense in equal measure about custom car building and full-size customs, Bob was always available to talk with other custom model car builders and was free with his candid opinions about custom auto styling.

Bob was one of my best friends in the hobby, and he will be remembered by model car builders everywhere as one of the leading spokesman of that segment of the model car hobby. Bob died in June 1994, but he left a legacy of work, ideas, ideals, and enthusiasm that continues to inspire not only my work, but that of many other builders of accurate custom models.

Bob Barnett
September 4, 1941–June 7, 1994

Foreword

Model building takes many forms and covers many subjects, depending on a builder's interests, skills, imagination and objectives.

As a scale vehicle modeler, your subject and style options are great. The amount of detail and complexity will vary with the builder and project. Out-of-the-box, kit-based, kitbashed, aftermarket-detailed or scratchbuilt—there is a building level for every interest and skill level. Curbside to contest caliber, large to small scales, a quick build for fun or a years-long replication project—the choice is yours. Some require effort to research and accurately capture the subject modeled at a particular point in time. For example, replica stock and accurate recreation of a specific 1:1 vehicle, whether it's one you own or use at work, a famous hot rod or race car, or a favorite custom you wish to render in scale requires skills, research, and attention to detail. These are all excellent disciplines to learn and draw from; they teach you to think, to see, and to figure out how to create a scale and convincing "reality," based on an actual vehicle.

But when you enter the arena of custom car modeling, based on your own ideas and vision of what the final project should contain and look like, you have an entire range of creativity before you. Mild or wild? Old or new? Classic, contemporary, or futuristic? You choose it, and you build it.

Mark S. Gustavson's love of and enthusiasm for hot rods and customs as modeling subjects is evident in his modeling projects over the years. A builder since the early 1960s, he has competed in and won local, regional, and national contests and has been a longtime advocate of accurate scale modeling stressing craftsmanship, precision, realism, and creativity. He has written this book for those of you who wish to build customs—whether as a first project or as part of your ongoing modeling interests—and want to know what techniques and procedures will be needed to create that vision in plastic.

The techniques depicted in this book apply to any plastic kit and often reflect the techniques and procedures commonly used in full-size customs of any era. You will find out how to perform simple to complex body modifications, from the basics of frenching an antenna to sectioning a body. Also covered are the planning and steps necessary to construct a realistic custom model that could actually be driven if built full size. Some of the procedures are easy; others are more challenging. But with care, patience, basic craftsmanship, and new skills developed through working with the examples and techniques shown in this book, you'll improve your finished models and take on more complex projects. This book, along with the many other excellent how-to books from Kalmbach, is filled with great ideas, useful information and handy tips, and will answer many of those "how did they do that?" questions.

I hope, as you read this book and try the techniques shown, you'll find that your modeling becomes more interesting and more fun. I also hope that you'll be inspired to construct a custom you've wanted to build for a long time, or to create a new project for your shelf or a contest.

—*Bob Wick*

Introduction

One of the most prominent, popular, and enduring segments of the automotive hobby is the design and construction of custom cars. At its best, a custom car reflects a personal sense of style and design and fulfills the creative need to restyle mass-produced automobiles to be more graceful and individual. By removing visual clutter, excess chrome, and out-of-proportion design elements that are often the result of marketing and production considerations, it is possible to create a more satisfying design than could be purchased in a showroom. Good automobile restyling takes a close look at what changes need to be made to achieve good overall design and proportions, integrated styling details, and more interesting visual elements. Typically, those alterations involve changing headlights, taillights, grilles, and bumpers, as well as more aggressive procedures like altering the basic proportions of the vehicle by chopping the top, sectioning the body, or lengthening or shortening fenders. Since not all changes are pleasing, thoughtful designers are careful to avoid making changes that do not improve the appearance of the car or that actually make things worse.

Originally the province of moneyed automobile owners who wished to drive cars with unique or different styling, customs (in the form of expensive coachbuilt cars) rolled from the shops of Bohman and Schwartz, Derham, Darrin, Fernandez, LeBaron, and others. However, the art of constructing custom automobiles became more democratic after World War II when a new crop of custom shops opened to serve a growing market that they helped create. Among the best were the Alexander Brothers, Joe Bailon, the Barris brothers, Clarkhaiser, Herschel "Junior" Conway, Bill Cushenberrry, Bill Hines, Rod Powell, Dave Puhl, Ed Roth, Doane Spencer, Darryl Starbird of Star Customs, Neil

One of the most famous of all custom vehicles is Spencer Murray's Dream Truck. Using the talents of almost a dozen gifted and competitive customizers in the '50s, it presaged later projects like Starbird's Predicta and Futurista, Cushenberry's Jade Idol, Winfield's Marquis and, later, Coddington's Cadzilla and Chezoom, Starbird's Debonair, and Trepanier's Sniper. Seen here in a never-before-published 1958 photograph taken just after the Truck was restyled for the last time before its catastrophic accident in Kansas in 1958, the Dream Truck was the first really high-profile custom. It set trends for 30 years. It has been restored and is now owned by custom car collector Kurt McCormick. Spencer Murray photo, Mark S. Gustavson photo archives

Starbird's Predicta is another epochal custom car. Based on a 1956 Thunderbird, this was the first privately constructed vehicle with a full bubble top. Darryl Starbird photo, Mark S. Gustavson photo archives

5

Emory and Clayton Jensen of Valley Custom, Joe Wilhelm, and Gene Winfield.

More recently, the work of a new breed of customizers has inspired a new generation and piqued the interest of old-timers. Creations from the workshops of Jim Bailie, Boyd Coddington, Frank DeRosa, John D'Agnostino, Larry Ericson, Greg Fluery, Sam and Chip Foose, Gary Howard, Larry Kramer, Howdy Ledbetter, Murphy and the Striper, Troy Trepanier, Elden Titus, Bill Reasoner, Mike Sydney, Jerry Sahagon, and others have furthered and reinvigorated the hobby by creating their own fresh visions of custom automobiles. Some of these customizers are from the first generation and still practice the art. Full-scale cars like the Cadzilla, the many customs of Richard Zoochi, Chezoom, Sniper, restored customs—including the Dream Truck, Jade Idol, and the Hirohata Mercury—the cloning of Valley Custom's Polynesian and Sam Barris' Buick, and the reappearance of well-designed and superbly executed custom cars at high-profile shows like the Grand National (Oakland) Roadster Show demonstrate that customizing has matured and will continue as an important part of the auto hobby.

The general popularity of custom cars has come, and gone, and returned over the last four decades, and is currently enjoying an unprecedented resurgence in interest among hobbyists. Model car customizing also reflects this resurgence of interest, with uncounted numbers of scale vehicle customs being constructed every year.

Sometimes considered to be one of the most advanced areas of the model car hobby, custom model car building is really no more difficult than building any other subset of automotive modeling subjects. Many of the basic construction techniques are straightforward and can be mastered if you have a good working knowledge of customizing procedures, tools, and techniques, mixed with patience and craftsmanship.

As the legendary designer Harry Bentley Bradley has pointed out, construction methods are the handmaiden to achieving a more beautiful and pleasing design. By mastering the techniques and styling considerations in this book, I hope that by designing and creating scale miniature custom cars you can help to preserve and advance the art of creating exciting and challenging scale miniature automotive customs.

Starbird has always coachbuilt the bodies for most of his show customs. The Forcasta, based on a 1960 Corvair, was a four-passenger street-driven custom with a large bubble covering four-passenger seating. This was a very high-profile custom car in the early '60s. Since restyled by a subsequent owner, it has lost most of its original charm. Darryl Starbird photo, Mark S. Gustavson photo archives

Another interesting vehicle is the famous Golden Nugget, now called Legacy after a subsequent modest restyling. Based on a 1967 Chevrolet, the car has a chopped '57 Buick roof, radically extended rear fenders, custom-built frame and a mildly sectioned body. Mark S. Gustavson photo archives

Customizing and Styling Glossary

"A" Pillar: The foremost pillar in the roof-to-body structure. Proceeding rearward, other pillars are labeled "B," "C," and, in station wagons, "D." Coupes typically have only "A" and "B" pillars.

"B" Pillar: Second pillar in the roof-to-body structure.

Backlight: The rear window of any automobile, regardless of body style.

Beltline: The horizontal line that separates the upper edge of the body where the vent, door, and quarter windows appear.

Bezel: A metal framework that surrounds a lamp or opening. Its finish may be chromed metal, polished stainless, or painted.

Body-on-Frame Construction: This is the traditional construction technique that places a body (consisting of all exterior body components, doors, quarter panels, roof, trunk, front fenders, hood, and the like) onto a separate frame to which all drivetrain and suspension components are attached. This technique is considered to be a strong and rigid approach to car construction, but it also produces a very heavy vehicle.

Bullnose: A streamlined thin ridge, running parallel to the car, along the hood. A traditional GM styling motif, pioneered by Harley Earl.

Center Line: The plane passing through the center of any component of the vehicle.

Channeling: Dropping the body over the frame rails to reduce the height of the body with respect to the ground. This is usually accomplished by cutting the flooring loose, moving it upward, and reattaching it to the body.

Character Line: A shape introduced to the body of the vehicle, whether incut or raised, that helps define or emphasize a particular design element of the vehicle (e.g., a taillight lens).

Chopping the Top: Dropping the height of the roof by removing a section of the "A," "B," and "C" pillars, where applicable. The glass height is also reduced by either reshaping the configuration of the windshield or backlight opening, or by removing a section of the glass.

Coke Bottle: In plan view, the center section of a car (through the door) is shorter than the height of the front clip and rear quarter panels. When viewed from above, the body is narrower in the middle section than over the front and rear wheels. This design idea was pioneered by GM's Bill Mitchell and Larry Shinoda.

Convertible Boot: A covering of vinyl or other similar material that hides the convertible top and its mechanisms.

Cowl: That portion of the body at the base of the windshield, including the vent panel for the defroster. The cowl does not extend into the adjoining left and right fender area.

Curb Height: The height of the vehicle at its uppermost portion, without passengers or trunk load.

Decked: Chrome removed from the trunk to achieve a smoothed look. Holes left by the molding are filled in and the entire panel is painted.

Decklid: A hinged panel providing access to the luggage compartment (usually called the trunk).

Dog Leg: A right-angle bend in any aspect of the vehicle.

Drip Molding: An exposed "L" channel placed over the door opening to direct water away from the windows and passengers. This molding also disguises the structural welding that attaches the roof to the body.

Fastback: A tapered roofline that slopes directly down toward or to the rear bumper of the vehicle.

Frenching: A term generally applied to the technique of welding a factory seam or removing a factory bezel in order to create a seamless, one-piece look. The goal is to remove all bezels and seams.

Front Clip: A term applied to the assembly of both front fenders, the hood, the grille, inner wheelhouse shapes, grille work and associated trim. Except in the case of a unibody design, these parts can be detached from the rest of the vehicle.

Gravel Deflector: A metal plate fitted between the front or rear bumper and the body.

Greenhouse: The upper body of an automobile, the structure above the beltline—glass, roof, and supporting structural members.

Grille: An ornament positioned in an opening at the front of an automobile, generally placed between the headlights, designed as decoration and to route air to the engine. Can be chromed metal, polished stainless steel, or painted body color. Typically, some sort of grid is installed within the circumference of the grille to exclude road debris from the radiator and other engine components.

Gutter: A channel for water drainage. Found in the opening around a hood, trunk, or door.

Hardtop: A term applied to any fixed roof with retracting window glass and no exposed "B" or middle pillar.

Header: The structural member above the windshield at the juncture with the forward edge of the roof panel.

Headliner: The material covering the roof inside a car, usually vinyl but sometimes cloth.

Hood: A hinged panel providing access to the engine compartment.

Lip Molding: A bright molding (stainless or anodized aluminum) applied to the body around the edge of a wheel opening.

Lower Back Panel: Portion of body sheet metal below the rear edge of the decklid and trunk.

Modesty Panel: Sheet metal below bumpers that conceals the frame. Can also apply to "ground effect" moldings fitted beneath a rocker molding or other panel.

Nosed: Chrome removed from hood. Holes left by discarded molding or nameplate are filled and entire panel is painted.

Overhang: The distance from the center line of wheels to the rearmost or foremost extension of the vehicle. See also "Ramp Angle."

Package Tray: The shelf in the interior between the top of the rear seat and the base of the backlight.

Pancaking: The technique that involves narrowing or shortening the shape of the hood, usually undertaken to introduce a new smoothed panel between the headlight or when reshaped fenders require the creation of a new hood shape. As the term implies, the hood usually ends up as a flat panel.

Quarter Panel: The rear fender or sheet-metal panel extending from the trailing edge of the door (whether two-door or four-door) to the rearmost extension of the bumper, taillight, or other part of the body. This panel also starts at the base of the backlight to the bottom of the panel and includes the rear wheel opening to the base of the roof and the trunk opening.

Ramp Angle: The angle created by lines tangent to the static loaded radii of front and rear wheels, converging at the point of lowest ground interference of the underside of the car.

Reveal Molding: A metal frame or molding outlining an opening or depression.

Rocker Panel: The sheet-metal surface below the door opening, running between the front and rear wheel openings.

Sectioning: The removal of a horizontal strip from the central point of an automobile body with the goal of reducing the overall height of the vehicle.

Scoop: A device to catch air; may be either functional or merely ornamental.

Scuff Plate: Cover over door sill, usually rubber or metal.

Spoiler: An air deflector typically applied to the rearmost upper edge of the trunk, extending sometimes to the top of the quarter panels.

Sugar Scoop: A depressed surface leading to an air scoop on the hood.

Tumblehome: The angle of the "B" pillar and side glass from the perpendicular at the beltline, as seen from front or rear.

Tunnel: The hump in the floor pan that provides clearance for the driveshaft.

Turnunder: Opposite of Tumblehome. The inward and downward sweep of sheet metal from the widest point on a car down to the rocker panel.

Unibody Construction: The near-universal modern assembly technique of mating the exterior body panels to a floorboard that doubles as a stressed "frame." To the integrated body-floorboard-frame assembly are bolted all drivetrain elements (engine, transmission, and so forth) as well as suspension components (upper and lower front suspension control arms, rear suspension leaf or coil springs, and other related parts). This construction technique is considered by some designers to be superior because the body panels are stressed structural members, allowing for more lightweight construction. It was first pioneered on the Tucker, then on the '58 Thunderbird/Lincoln, then, more generally, on the 1960 Falcon and Comet, the 1962 Fairlane, the 1964 Mustang II, the 1969 Maverick, and other vehicles.

Wheelbase: The distance between the front and rear axle, expressed in inches.

Window Molding: Any molding that frames the window of a vehicle; usually stainless steel or bright-dip anodized aluminum. In modern vehicles, these moldings are painted dark gray or body color.

Z'ed: When metal is added to a frame, or when it is cut or rewelded, to allow the frame to drop the axles (under the floorpan) to be closer to the ground. This lowers the car body without changing suspension geometry and keeps the vertical interior room (headroom) stock. Usually done on older cars with full frames (pre-unibody).

one

Basic Supplies and Techniques

Before you start your project, let's discuss the tools and supplies you will need. The right tools will permit you to do things you might not have thought possible—and to do them more easily and efficiently than you might have imagined. We'll also explore some basic techniques that, once mastered, will allow you to work through your favorite custom project without difficulty or disappointment.

While you can spend a lot of money on tools (and you may eventually decide to acquire some expensive equipment like a mill and a lathe, a media blasting cabinet, and a nickel-plating setup), you can get started relatively cheaply. Visit a good hobby shop and buy the best-quality products, right from the start. There is no substitute for good equipment and supplies.

Finally, you need to become conversant with the lexicon of auto body design and customizing. Please study the Glossary (page 7) so that when technical terms are used in the following chapters, you'll understand them readily.

Hobby knife and blades. The most basic of all model car equipment, this tool can be used for a wide range of tasks. There are several kinds of handles on the market. Purchase the most

Mercari by Mark S. Gustavson

expensive one you can and be aware that it will last no more than a few months of hard use. Buy your no. 11 hobby blades in quantity (you can buy as many as 100 to a package). This is the most economical way, and it will keep you from running back to the hobby store in the middle of a project. Prepare to buy new handles frequently.

Hobby files. Hobby files are essential to shaping body parts. They ensure that the new shape is true and devoid of unsightly dips and other surface irregularities. You will need basic flat files that can be purchased in sets at hobby stores or through Harbor Freight outlets. These shapes are flat (the one you'll use most), round (the next most frequently used shape), and angled (e.g., triangles and the like). You also need a set of good riffler files—these bent files permit you to get into recessed areas into which a standard flat file won't fit.

You will also need a file card. Remember that files do their work by scraping away material, and the fine serrations on the face of a file can get clogged. Rather than throw away expensive files after they become filled with material, you can clean them out by gently drawing a file card across a file, in several different directions, until the material has been removed. Keep in mind, though, that files do get dull and eventually have to be replaced.

Strip styrene. This product comes in various shapes. Purchase a wide selection. Evergreen brand is the best. Strip styrene can be used to create custom side trim, to reinforce panels after sectioning, and for other customizing tasks.

Hobby saws. You will have to cut parts to build a custom model car. Hobby saws will permit you to cut styrene, resin, or brass with a clean, straight line, burr free. Buy the best fine-tooth saws available, in both deep and shallow blade configurations. Keep the blades away from water and never use oil on them as a lubricant; it would interfere with your use of adhesive and paint.

Scribes, tweezers, and scissors. Whenever you cut across a panel line (door, trunk, and so forth), you will need to reestablish the line. You will also need to clean out such lines right before painting so that the finish coats won't fill them up, making the model unrealistic.

As with other tools, there are several shapes of scribes for every application. You can obtain these scribes from Micro-Mark or a dental supply business.

Dremel tools with accessories. Though entry-level model car customizing doesn't require the use of a Dremel tool, there are times when only a rotating shaping bit will accomplish a task. For instance, when you have flared a fender and you want to reduce the thickness of the fender at the wheel well, using a round cutter head in your motor tool (set at a low speed) will allow you to thin that fender lip. Similarly, you can gently grind away the thin skiff of putty that you have applied to the inside of your latest top-chopping project.

For tight spaces, consider one of the flexible shaft attachments so you can access the restricted areas.

Adhesives. Unless you have moved on to brass fabrication, you must find a foolproof plastic glue. Historically, modelers have used tube- or bottle-type glues. However, except for very limited applications where the solvent action can work to help you form a rounded shape (see Chapter Five), these adhesives are not strong enough.

Two major kinds of adhesives are preferred by the better builders. First are the two-part epoxies (there are many suitable brands), which are best used to strengthen joints and as fillers inside weak panels. Two-part epoxy adhesives are suitable neither for delicate work nor to join together joints or parts that will appear on the outside of a model.

Second, instant-type glues are ideal. They can set up instantly with the use of an accelerant. These adhesives can be purchased in gap-filling or the thinner, waterlike versions. You can apply them with the narrow spout of the bottle, but better yet, use a toothpick or the tip of a hobby knife so that it gets exactly where it should be. Beware of one problem with this material, however; it is considerably harder than the surrounding plastic surfaces, so you must use great care and the right materials to smooth down surfaces on which it appears. Never use coarse sandpaper to smooth down a joint on which cured instant adhesive has spilled. A flat file or a coarse sanding stick, applied flat across the glue joint, will level the surface of two different materials.

Avoid the fumes of an instant glue. They can seriously irritate your eyes. And use latex gloves (not absorbent cotton gloves) when applying the accelerant (which is mostly formaldehyde) because this chemical has been linked to a range of long-exposure disorders.

Sandpaper and sanding sticks. No matter what you do, sooner or later you will have to use some sanding medium to smooth down your work, and you must use supplies that will permit you to true the surface for a flawless finish.

When sanding a large surface on which putty has been applied, fold over a piece of 220-grit autobody paper and knock down the putty to a rough contour. Then, grab a fresh coarse sanding stick and use it to do the finish sanding and shaping of your flat or contoured panels. Rather than sand in just one direction, place the sanding stick parallel to the longest dimension of your panel and then move it at an angle approximating 30 degrees to the length of the model. Then reverse the angle. This will avoid sanding a flat spot into your panel but will remove the irregularities. See Illustration 8A, page 82.

Putty. Avoid lacquer- or solvent-based putties for anything other than filling nicks or other *very* small surface flaws. These products dry by evaporating the solvents and often continue to soften the plastic and primer later, causing dips and other surface flaws. Though there are several two-part epoxy putties that produce good results, I prefer autobody products. If used properly, they can produce splendid results. In my opinion, the best product for filling in small

1 You can use a hobby knife, turned around, to clean the primer, sanding residue, or putty from a door line or other panel line. Start off by applying gentle pressure, and don't try to remove all of the crud in one pass. By slightly angling the blade, you can slightly widen the panel line to anticipate the line-narrowing effect of primer and paint.

2 You can also emphasize the appearance of certain styling elements of a model. In this case, we are highlighting the drip rail by scoring a defining line underneath it.

3 Another use for an old hobby blade is to apply very small bits of spot putty to fill in a deep sanding scratch. Lay the blade at a shallow angle to the surface so that the putty can be applied smoothly.

Quick Tip

Be very careful if you have to pull a hobby knife toward you. Also, keep your hands out of the way of the path of the blade when you are working on your custom project. Respect these blades because they are surgically sharp and you can get a nasty cut faster than you'd think.

4 You can also create a new panel line. In this case, let's create a rounded door corner. First draw the shape with a pencil and then . . .

5 . . . make a series of gentle scribe lines around the radius of your new panel line. You should make many passes with the hobby knife rather than one deep scribe.

gaps and doing other customizing tasks is Evercoat Euro-soft polyester putty. You use it by mixing a small quantity of a catalyst with the putty, thereby triggering a curing process that does not depend upon solvents to work. You can buy it from any business selling autobody products, but be sure to insist upon the Euro-soft version. This putty is dimensionally stable—it won't shrink once it sets up. It is strong and can be sanded to a sharp edge. However, it is best not to apply it over any kind of primer (enamel or lacquer). Once it is sanded, subsequent primer coats can create an embossed shape that is difficult to remove and tends to appear in your final paint job as a "ghost" image. Therefore, it is best to follow the techniques of custom autobody experts: first do all your work in the base material (in our case, usually styrene); then do all of your putty work; and then and only then apply primer, later sealer, and then your color and clear coats. Be completely satisfied with the basic custom work before you apply the first coat of primer. Use primer only to fill in minor sanding scratches and other inconsequential surface defects.

Rough-shape your catalyzed polyester putty before it hardens. Use an old hobby blade to reduce the work necessary to smooth the surface.

Toothbrush. A toothbrush is essential to good craftsmanship. When you are finished sanding your model, use an old soft toothbrush to gently remove sanding debris from panel lines and recessed areas of your model. You can use it wet or dry, but it is important to eliminate all unwanted materials from your model before applying another coat of primer or a color coat.

Profile tool and calipers. One of the hardest obstacles to overcome is the prospect of nonsymmetrical features on your model. You can imagine the typical problems:

your newly sectioned body is shorter on one side than the other or the reshaped roof is lopsided.

There are some simple ways to sidestep this problem. First, before you reattach parts to one another, use calipers (you can purchase inexpensive ones at a hobby store) to check and recheck every measurement. Establish a common point of reference to check the dimensions of all parts, especially after you tentatively reattach them.

Additionally, once you have rough-sanded a part to shape, use a profile tool to see if one side matches the other. Use it gently so you don't gouge the surface.

Another way to check out a shape is to make a tracing of a wheel well opening and then cut away the body part, leaving only the wheel well shape, for instance. After making the tracing, flip it around and compare it to the shape on the other side.

Safety equipment (masks and gloves and eye protection). It is essential to isolate your lungs from sanding and paint materials. When you are sanding catalyzed putty, wear a simple dust mask to avoid inhaling the small dust particles. When you apply any type of paint (lacquer, enamel, water-based, urethane), you must use a double-cartridge respirator.

Get some kind of qualified eye protection. The threats to your eyesight are manifold: a tool flipping into your eyes, a bit of plastic spinning off a motor tool, fumes from instant glue, a chip of putty kicked up in a sanding operation. Buy some safety glasses and use them. You can't be any kind of modeler if you can't see.

Finally, use latex gloves when you apply an accelerant to instant glue. Formaldehyde does not occur ordinarily in everyday experience, and your skin is a poor barrier to the assimilation of this and other dangerous chemicals.

6 Differently shaped hobby files can emphasize or create a body line. Here, the sharp tip of a square hobby file highlights a character line inside the grille opening on this frenched '58 Thunderbird front grille.

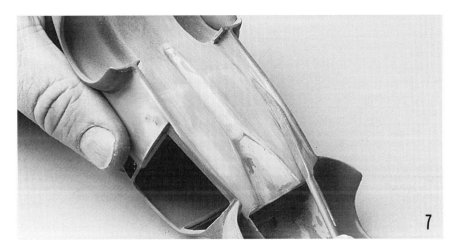

7 Riffler files have a wide range of applications. Because of their shape, you can get them into recessed areas that a traditional hobby file can't reach.

8 Files come in several shapes and sizes. You can purchase files from a hobby store, by mail order, or through a discount business like Harbor Freight. Also get a file card (seen here on the right) to clean your files of debris.

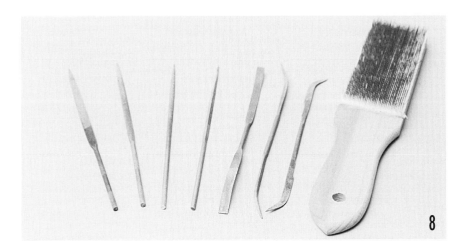

9 Strip styrene comes in many shapes and is literally indispensable to the model car customizer. Acquire a range of strips for your customizing.

10 One essential task is reinforcing panels that you have cut apart. Here, you must first rout out a recess into which the strip styrene can be fitted. In this case, a round cutter has been fitted to a motor tool and then passed along the previously glued joint. Be careful to maintain a uniform width and depth. Clean up the rough routing with a square riffler file.

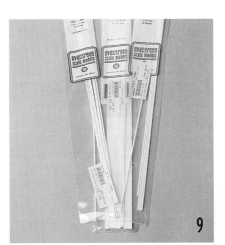

Quick Tips

Once you have your tools and supplies, it is important to keep them very clean. After each use, thoroughly scour them of debris, putty, and other junk. Replace worn hobby blades with new ones as you clean up after each work session. Nothing is more annoying than to be working hard on a new customizing project and have to stop and clean your equipment.

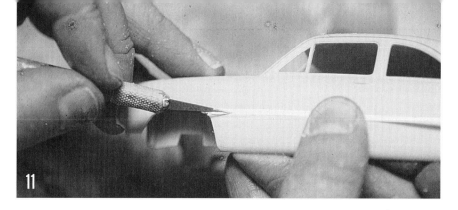

11 Apply a thin bead of instant glue into the trough you made in the previous strip and then press the strip styrene into the void, which is just wider and deeper than the shape of your strip styrene. Strip styrene bridges the joint, strengthens the body, and eliminates a lot of body work later on.

12 Once the instant adhesive has set up, sand the surface with 220-grit autobody paper to smooth it. In this case, we are trying to preserve the gentle curve of the side; therefore, we use no files or sanding sticks.

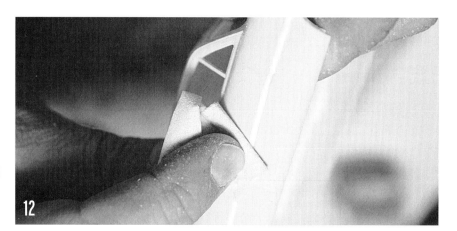

13 Apply a thin coat of catalyzed polyester putty over the joint with an old hobby knife. When it has cured, rough up the surface with some 220 paper, then use a coarse sanding stick, "rocked" around the radius of the shape, to smooth the side of the body.

14 Hobby saws come in different configurations. Use the shorter saw for areas where a smaller saw is necessary.

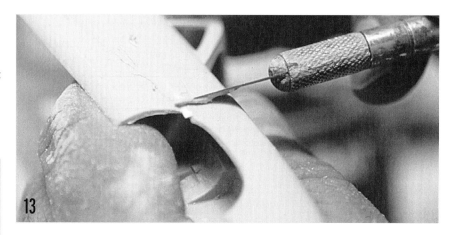

Quick Tip

Make sure that the entire length of the strip styrene has been completely attached by your instant adhesive.

Instead of laminating a series of thin or narrow strips (depending on the application) to form a larger shape, consider using a larger piece of strip styrene. File it roughly to shape before attaching it to your model. The resulting assembly with be much stronger.

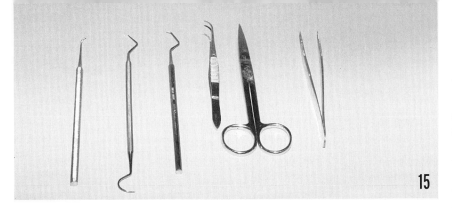

15 All of these tools, from scribes on the left to scissors and tweezers, are useful to the custom model car builder.

16 A hobby saw has uncounted uses in model car customizing. Choose a fine-blade saw, in several different saw depths, to maximize the number of applications. In this photo, a hobby blade saws through a '50 Chevy pickup cab during sectioning. Keep the blade square to a perpendicular line drawn through the object of your work.

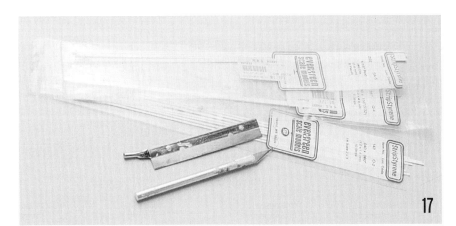

17 A hobby saw can also trim strip styrene to length. Make small cuts to ensure the accuracy of your work and to protect you from injury.

18 Use a scribe to clean out a panel line, to sharpen an intersection between two parts, or for any one of a hundred other reasons.

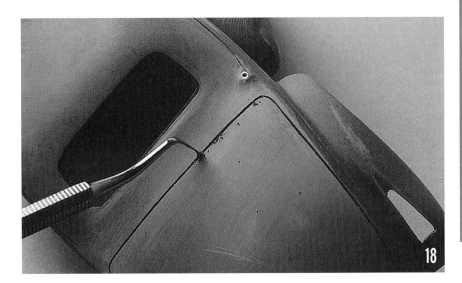

Quick Tips

Depending on the application, an angle cut may be stronger than a right-angle butt joint.

Make sure that all your joints are full contact, rather than crude joints in which the gap is filled with adhesive.

When doing any custom body work, do both sides at the same time to minimize the possibility of getting different results because you forgot about a procedure or technique. Uniformity is a goal.

Make several smaller passes rather than one or a few really deep, dramatic cuts. Be careful with these tools—they are very sharp.

Try to move the scribe away from you to help prevent injury.

19 The motor tool is almost indispensable to the model car customizer. You can purchase the battery-powered one on the left or the traditional one on the right. They are virtually indestructible with reasonable care, and their wide array of cutters will allow you to handle any imaginable task.

20 A wide range of adhesives and solvents is available to the model car customizer. From the left, here are the universally useful instant adhesive with accelerant, two-part epoxy, and one kind of solvent.

21 A Dremel tool will allow you to thin out an inner fender to achieve a better sense of scale thickness. Or you can use it to shape a fender or rout out a proposed headlight or taillight recess.

Quick Tips

Be careful about which cutter you use. If you want to thin a panel, use a large round head to knock down a volume of material without cutting through the panel. Consider using a smaller round cutter only after removing most of the material. Preferably, however, use a piece of 220-grit sandpaper to clean up the cutter lines.

Depending on the application, consider using an elliptically shaped cutter to remove the desired material.

19

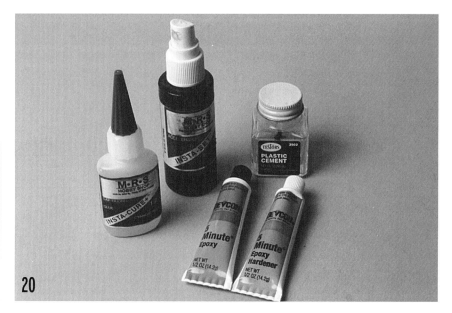

20

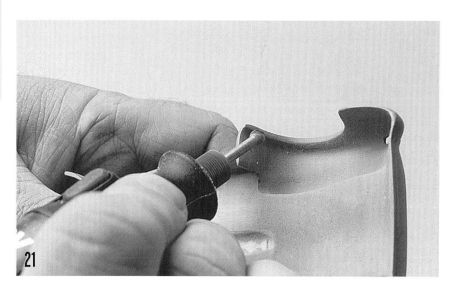

21

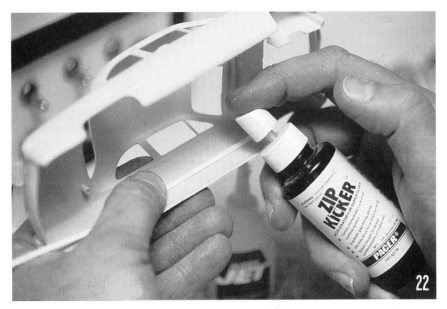

22 Once the instant glue has been applied, a quick and modest shot of accelerant or baking soda will set up the instant glue more quickly, and enhance the strength of the joint.

23 There are a lot of abrasives available these days to the hobbyist. In the background is a piece of 3M brand 360-grit wet-and-dry sandpaper. Diagonally is a piece of 220-grit long board auto-body paper, with the revolutionary sanding sticks on the right. Use autobody paper. Non-auto sandpapers "load up" too quickly and produce deep scratches on your model that are hard to remove. Proceed from coarse to medium to fine sandpaper and sanding sticks. In this way, you can achieve a smoother surface. Also, use sanding sticks whenever you can—they work as block sanding for the body work.

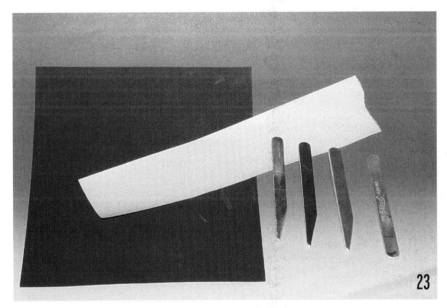

24 When you prepare your model for paint, use only the very fine autobody sandpapers. You can get papers that range from 600 to 2000 grit. Don't be fooled by competitive papers—3M brand and equivalent sandpapers are correctly formulated for professional paint jobs, so use them!

Quick Tips

Avoid the solvent-based glues because they take a long time to dry and they soften the plastic. Use an adhesive that sets up catalytically (like a standard so-called instant glue augmented by an accelerant). Use a two-part epoxy when you need to strengthen a joint (like one produced by sectioning or chopping) in conjunction with a strip of styrene or thin brass strip.

25 Probably the best filler these days is the Evercoat brand Euro-soft polyester putty. It sets up with a catalyst, is strong, won't bleed through any overcoat primer or paint, and can be sanded to a sharp edge. It won't soften plastic or create sink marks at any time.

25

26 Mixing and applying this product isn't difficult. First, drop a bit onto a bit of putty onto a smooth surface. A piece of slick paper works well. Use only enough catalyst to moderately tint the putty; it should "kick" in about 3 to 4 minutes.

26

27 Thoroughly mix the two products together and then apply with an old hobby knife.

27

28 An old soft toothbrush is an essential tool. Gently run the bristles along panel lines, in recesses, or underneath hard-to-reach shapes (like fenders) to ferret out sanding residue and other debris. You can also use the toothbrush wet by applying a bit of liquid dishwashing soap to the brush, and gently scrubbing down the entire model. Never use a toothbrush for personal hygiene once you have used it on your project.

Quick Tips

Avoid using solvent-based putties. They are little more than thick lacquer primer and they will soften the plastic, causing the plastic to shrink and sag, thereby ruining body work.

Do all of the plastic and putty work before you prime your model. Primer should be used to detect moderate or fine surface flaws and should not be used to detect gross errors.

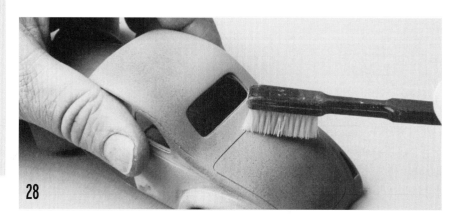
28

29

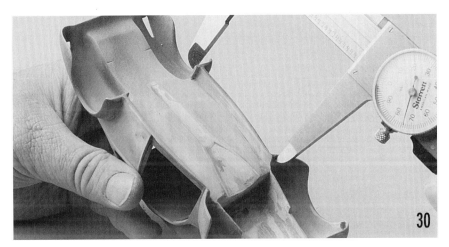

30

31

32

Quick Tips

When using the Profile tool, press gently to be sure that the shape is correctly presented as each wire is pushed through the center section. Also, be sure that you flip the shape around for the other side since each side is the mirror image of the other.

29 A profile tool will ensure that one side of a project matches the other. Gently press it against the finished bodywork or over the first coat of primer to develop a profile. Then flip the tool around and apply it to the other side of the bodywork, at exactly the same place, to see if your work has been uniform.

30 Use calipers constantly to measure your work before you make a cut, before you use an adhesive, and after the body is roughly assembled.

31 Buy and use a good-quality respirator. Purchase one with replaceable canisters and replace them regularly. Between uses, store it in a plastic bag.

32 The other critical safety measure is good eye protection. Use glasses whenever you work on your models.

Quick Tips

Be careful not to use a new brush, or an old brush with stiff bristles. The point here is to remove debris from your model, not to scratch the surface.

Be careful if you use a toothbrush to remove color sanding or polishing muck from panel lines. A polished paint surface (whether enamel or lacquer) is quite a bit more delicate than a primed model.

two

How to Chop a Top and Create New Glass

Among the tricks that customizers have used, few are as dramatic as the decision to lower the height of the roof, measured as that part of the body between the belt line to the top of the roof. This styling decision can, if used carefully and with restraint, streamline a design by removing an out-of-proportion design element.

By carefully considering the styling of the top chop on your model, you will design a custom model car that could be driven and operated safely. As with other aspects of model car customizing, do some drawings—try to visualize how the final design will appear. And remember not to remove too much height from the roof; as the architect Ludwig Mies van der Rohe advised, less is more.

In this case, let's chop the top on our project 1940 Ford coupe. Lowering the roof on a vehicle with a sloping roof, like the '40 Ford, presents some interesting design challenges; if it's poorly done, the model might lack a graceful resolution between the roof and other body panels or might wind up with a flattop that is unpleasant from a design standpoint.

1951 Chevy by Ken Hamilton

1 Any model with a sloping top can be chopped using the techniques here. Note the subtle chop on the model in the foreground and how the area of the roof just above and to the rear of the rear quarter window has been leaned forward a bit to avoid getting a hip at the rear of the roof. The goal is to gracefully drop the height of a roof. This time, we will take a bit more out of the roof and take a fresh run at keeping the windows big and airy.

2 To make the process easier, remove the drip rails with a flat file. After that, sand the filed areas with 220-grit sandpaper or a medium sanding stick.

3 The '90 Ford top looks best when the backlight is leaned forward to avoid the flattop look that so often occurs during chopping: the roof must flow gracefully and smoothly into the tulip panel and trunk. Use a pencil to mark the cut surrounding the rear window. (Never use a felt-tip marker.) The width of the area should extend around about half the radius of the side of the roof. This will make the job easier later on.

4 To accomplish the chop, we will cut the A, B, and C pillars. First, mark the C pillar as shown (marked part B here). Mark the line across the side of the roof to the window edge to reshape the C pillar on the body as it adjoins the rear window. Remember to make as few cuts as possible—so plan what you are going to do. Duplicate the B shape on the other side of the body. Note also that we have marked the B pillars (both sides) and the A pillars. These cut lines should be about halfway up the length of the pillar through the flattest (least angled) area of each pillar.

5 Using a fine-tooth hobby saw, start your cut across the top of the roof on both lines above and below part A. Proceed with great care to avoid injury and to minimize the width of the cut. Saw completely across the roof to the upper line of part B and all the way through the roof.

Quick Tips

Make as few cuts as you possibly can.

Always bevel the intersection between adjoining custom panels to permit your putty to bridge the gap and reduce the chance that the bodywork will appear through your custom paint job.

Use only instant adhesive, with accelerator. Never use a solvent glue for this task.

Use a template to check your work constantly.

Use calipers to check your work.

Illustration 2A

Tulip panel

Backlight

Create a smooth transition between base of backlight and tulip panel.

Trunk line

Avoid a "hip" in the transition between base of backlight and tulip panel.

6 With the first two cuts out of the way, it is time to free up the backlight panel. Install a fresh no. 11 blade in your handle and start to scribe a series of light cuts, each one a little deeper than the proceeding one, until the backlight panel is freed. True both sides of the cut lines by gently passing a flat hobby file over both surfaces of the part just cut loose. Be careful not to make the cut any longer than your pencil-marked shape is.

7 Remove the back panel and set it aside for now: there is a lot more work to do before we reinstall this part!

8 With the backlight panel severed, it is time to cut loose the rear side of the roof panels. Once again, make your cuts straight and don't rush the job. Make the bottom cut even with the bottom of the base line of the rear quarter window, as shown here, and then make the final cut at the top of the C pillar, too. Repeat this process on the other side. You should now have three parts so far: the wide backlight piece and two roof side parts. Set them aside for now.

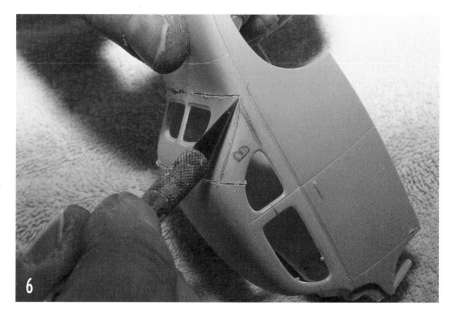

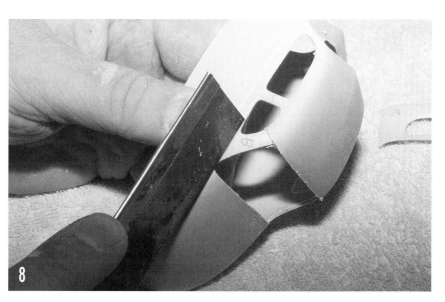

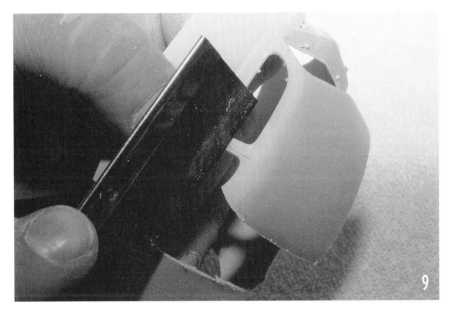

9 After severing the C pillars on both sides of the body, cut the B and A pillars. Use your fine-tooth hobby saw gently because you don't want to tear the pillars loose from the body.

10 If you have done your work carefully, all the pillars will be of the same length, using a line drawn horizontally across the roof under the side glass sill as the benchmark.

11 Using as much care as possible, shorten the A and B pillars by approximately 3/32″. Make the cuts straight and use the same fine-tooth hobby saw. All four cuts should be made at this time; when you're finished, set the roof on a flat surface and make sure that all four pillars touch the table and that the cuts are all the same length.

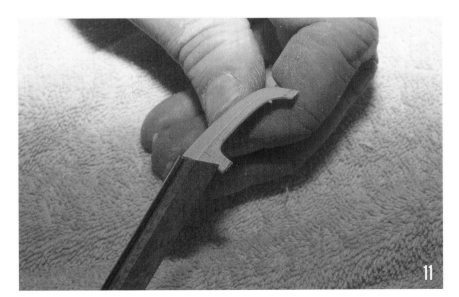

12 Next, remove ⁷⁄₁₆″ from the trailing edge of the roof. This will shorten the top and permit us to tip the backlight panel forward. It is hard to anticipate precisely how much to remove. But since it is not difficult to install a filler panel, the most important thing is to get the shape right.

13 Now, start to put the model back together. Carefully line up the A pillars; using instant adhesive liberally on both the A and B pillars, rejoin them. Don't worry about the mismatched B pillars and don't cut across the top to stretch out the roof so they line up. It is a lot less work to reshape the B pillars than to add styrene across the roof.

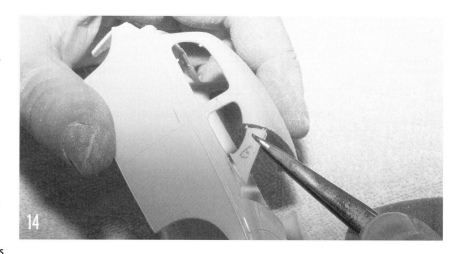

14 Measure several times to make sure the backlight body section is square on the body: it is essential that this panel be glued squarely so the roof panel is straight side to side and top to bottom. Now determine the angle of the backlight panel with respect to the body and the previously reattached roof. Try to imagine the final shape of the roof when considering where to reattach the backlight panel. There are no hard and fast rules here; good taste and esthetic judgment are important elements of customizing. In this case, note that an angle sympathetic to the side cut of the backlight panel has been filed into the body.

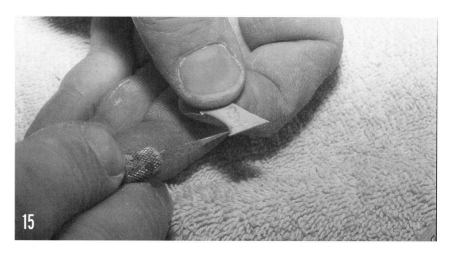

15 Now reshape the C pillars so they will fit neatly. File the bottom and top of this shape so it fits as neatly as possible into the hole in the body. Measure carefully by holding the part up to the body, and mark a line along the bottom to increase its angle. This will appear to lower the height of the quarter window too much, but that can be fixed later. Repeat the procedure on both sides so they are identical.

16 Note how part B fits flush with the body. Fashion a filler of styrene to fill the gap between the trailing edge of the roof and the leading edge of the backlight panel. I used Evergreen strip styrene, ³⁄₃₂″ thick. I shaped it with my fingers and needle-nose pliers. You will need to fit, file, and refit this piece repeatedly until it fits neatly.

17 Install the filler piece into the gap; use liberal amounts of gap-filling instant adhesive with some accelerator. How you install the filler styrene determines the basic shape of the newly-crafted roof: the top of the insert is roughly level with roof. You can always grind out excess material from underneath the roof. Use a round file to shape the area so the curve of the roof flows gently into the backlight: the goal is to shape the top so the roof flows neatly into the tulip panel. Avoid getting a hip into the body (see Illustration 2A).

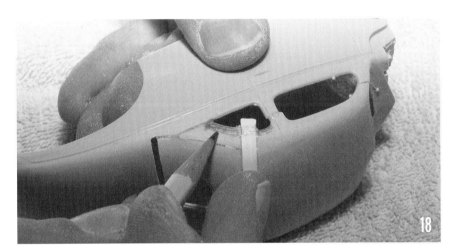

18 To keep the top from being too heavy, let's raise the side windows to create a larger opening. This will make the model more realistic and relieve the heavy overhang that typically appears on these Fords when the top is chopped. Mark a new window shape with a pencil.

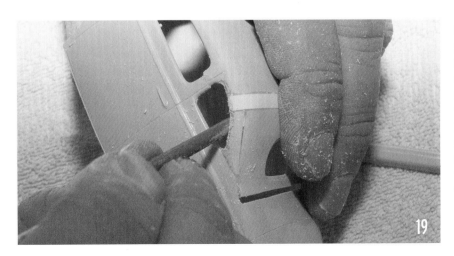

19 Use a half-round hobby file to remove the material marked in the previous step. Carefully remove only the targeted material. With the basic shape cut, use a half-round or elliptical file and clean up the area. Shape the area with care and don't remove too much material. Make sure you don't file the outside of the window opening wider than the innermost part of it. Repeat the step for the other side.

20 Repeat this procedure in the door window glass opening. The upper elevation of the door window glass opening should be level with the upper elevation of the quarter window glass area. The goal here is to raise the windows to lighten up the design and achieve a lithe, airy look. Mail-slot windows make no practical sense and are not esthetically pleasing. Also install a bit of strip styrene to the B pillar so that the pillars, on both sides of the door line, are parallel. This is much easier than slicing the roof another time and installing another strip of styrene just to line up the B pillar.

21 Now fill in the gap at the base of the backlight panel and the tulip panel. Choose an appropriate thickness of strip styrene, file it to shape, and install it with plenty of gap-filling instant adhesive.

22 When the adhesive is cured, file it to shape. This time, use a half round file, because the goal here is to create a gentle curve from the roof to the backlight to the tulip panel to the trunk. Grab a coarse sanding stick and thoroughly sand the entire roof to true up the reworked areas. This procedure will also provide a good bite for the primer to follow. Up to this point, not a spot of putty has been necessary.

23 It is important to clean up the shapes of the side windows. Determine what shape you would like to feature on the rear quarter window and make a template from paper. Then transfer the shape to a piece of .015 sheet styrene. Using the lower front side of the quarter window shape as the benchmark, use the template to trace the desired shape onto the body. Then, using small hobby files, modify the roughed-in quarter window shape until it matches the template. Repeat for the other side.

24 Repeat step 22 for the door window opening, too. Make sure that the bottom of the window glass is parallel with and matches the bottom of the quarter window shape. Repeat for the other side, using a benchmark. Note that just a spot of 3M Acryl red has been used to correct some very minor surface irregularities in the B pillar shape.

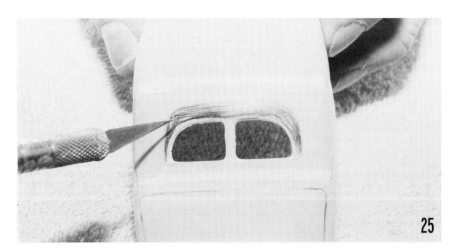

25 At this stage, let's enlarge the rear window to relieve some of the tomblike feeling of the Ford model. Since it is not much of a problem to cut glass from clear styrene stock, you have a lot of freedom to make windows in whatever shape you please. Pencil in your design and then look at it from every angle, including the side, to see how an open area can fit into the overall design. In this case, the backlight will be part of the sweep of the roof design. Again, use a pencil and draw your shape. In this case, we will remove the factory split window feature.

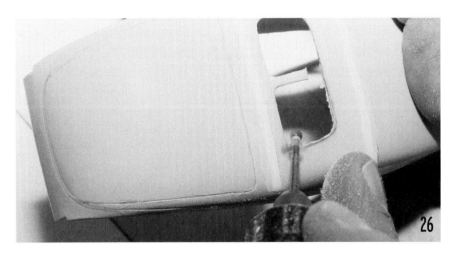

26 Rout out the area using standard customizing techniques discussed. Just remember to always wear eye protection and proceed slowly.

27 Once you have created the basic shape, clean up the roughness created by the cutter with a piece of folded 220-grit autobody paper, used dry. Go slowly.

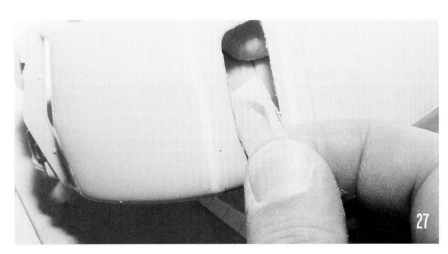

28 Note that a template is being made here. Trace the opening on one side of the window (the one you like best) onto a bit of card stock, cut out the shape and fit that template into the opening on the first side to check the fit. Fit the template into the opening at a right angle to the actual plastic, rather than behind it. Reverse the template and check the other side. Do whatever shaping is necessary.

29 Here's another trick to integrate the design. Instead of reinstalling the drip rails, cut a new reveal line into the body in order to tie together the upper door line and the newly-shaped trunk line. This is easy to do: just draw the line with a pencil, and then use a hobby knife and scribe the line. Remember to think creatively about new ways to integrate panel lines and shapes.

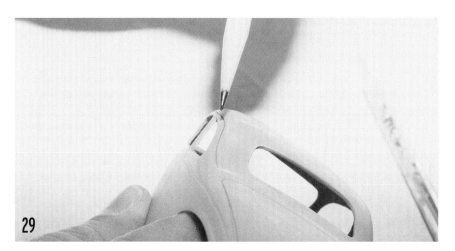

30 Use your surface template to check both sides of the model to insure uniformity. Always check and recheck the shapes and measurements of your work so that the completed model will stand up to the closest scrutiny.

31 Once you have established the shape of your windshield and backlight openings, it's time to make up a window channel and some "glass." Take a look at Illustration 2B for one way to build a glass channel. Depending on the style you choose, you'll have to cut down some old kit glass. (Of course, you could cut some clear acetate.) Find some clear plastic from your parts box that generally matches the curvature of your custom body. You can cut the glass with a fine-tooth hobby saw.

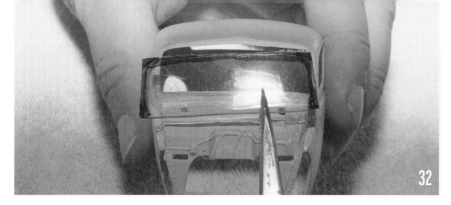

32 Using a marker pen, trace the outline onto your glass shape so that cutting the outline will be easier to do. Remember to mark the shape larger than necessary—you can always remove additional material, but you can never add any! Once the basic shape has been achieved by sawing, get out a coarse sanding stick or a small flat hobby file to fine-tune the shape. Progress to a medium, then a fine, sanding stick. Constantly recheck the glass to the window opening.

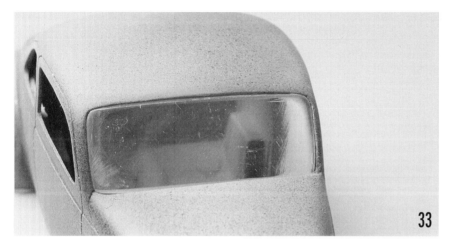

33 With a lot of patient, careful work, you can adapt a section of glass from another kit to fit quite tightly. Once the window is roughed in, as it is here, don't do any final polishing until the model is painted—the thickness of the paint will almost certainly require the removal of a little more glass material. Once the glass is fitted to the painted and polished body, sand the visible surfaces with 2000-grit 3M paper and then polish with Meguiar's Plexiglas polish. In this application, a very thin diameter wire (.015) will be fit around the interface between the outer diameter of the glass and the inner diameter of the body to simulate modern glass installation designs.

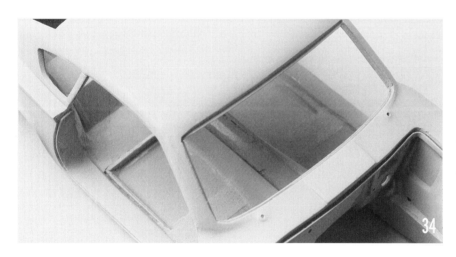

34 Another way to accomplish the same task is to create a right-angle brass channel, instant-glue it to the body, fit the glass, then create some special photoetched trim that will straddle the interface between the glass and the body (see Illustration 2B). In this application for my model of the lost Lincoln-Mercury dream car, the Lynx, two-level photocut trim will simulate the traditional Ford stainless molding/rubber channel. One of the several chemical darkening liquids that can be airbrushed will achieve the appearance of the debossed inner rubber molding.

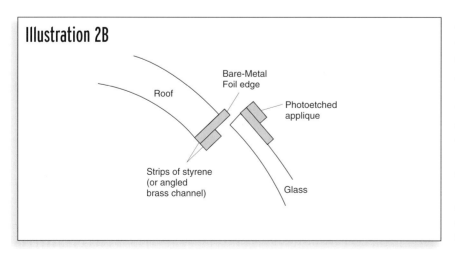

Illustration 2B

Roof

Bare-Metal Foil edge

Photoetched applique

Strips of styrene (or angled brass channel)

Glass

three

The Joys of Sectioning

Another dramatic and effective restyling technique is to remove a horizontal section from around the circumference of the body. If done carefully and with an eye to good design, sectioning your car can introduce a better balance between the height of the roof and the height of the body. Like other customizing procedures, this must be used with restraint. Usually, just a subtle sectioning will be enough to bring the body into better proportion.

Removing too much material will make the body too short for a human being to comfortably sit in or operate the vehicle. Remember, good customizing (in whatever scale) includes giving consideration to the real-world operation of the vehicle. For instance, the front wheels must have enough room to have full vertical travel and rotational arc. Additionally, a real human being must be able to get in and out of the car and operate it safely. Practical problems like these not only spoil an otherwise interesting design, but tell the viewer that the designer and builder really didn't give enough thought to practical considerations.

To achieve a good result, again, make a drawing and think about the practical aspects of your design.

Frank Olsen's replica of Pat Mulligan's '58 Chevrolet

1 With the top chopped modestly, it is time to modify the body to bring it into proportion. Our '40 Ford will benefit from about a 3 scale inch section job. Using ⅛″ tape, define the horizontal material to be removed by applying the tape as shown. In this case, the subject area is not only the most vertical part of the body, but it is the area where the body could most benefit from a reduction in height. Make sure to test-fit the body to the fender assembly so that you can mark the hood correctly when it is in the correct position. Make sure to apply the tape identically to both sides of the body—it is crucial that both sides be symmetrical.

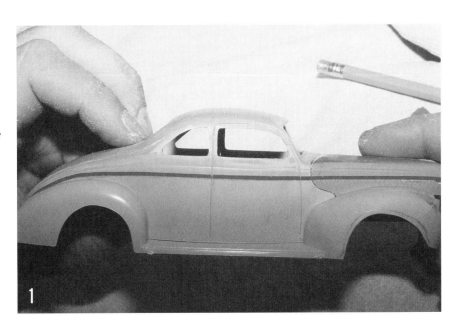

2 After removing the body from the fender assembly, note that the tape line is above the rear fender cutout area. You do not want to cut into that area and lose the radius. When you cut through this area, use a panel scriber or a hobby blade to scribe the two lines (on the top and bottom of the tape line).

3 Start to make the cut by using a fine-tooth hobby saw on the top of the tape line. Make sure that you work slowly and carefully to avoid having the saw blade wander either wide of or into the taped area. A successful result depends upon very careful work— take your time for best results.

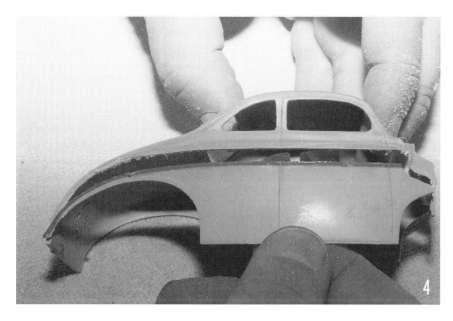

4 If you have worked carefully, the top of the body, including around the radius of the rear wheel cutout area, should be removed at this point. Repeat the procedure on the other side of the body. Once again, work slowly and be patient.

5 Repeat the process by slicing the body on the bottom of the tape line applied earlier. Since this part is more fragile than the entire body assembly was when you made the first cut, you will have to be very careful to avoid breaking the lower body part. Repeat the procedure on the other side of the body.

6 After you have trued the top and bottom body halves, it is time to rejoin the body panels. Using a liberal amount of instant adhesive, with an accelerator, attach the two body parts together. Repeat for the other side. When the adhesive has kicked or cured, it is time to reinforce the body to prevent cracking later on. Refer to Illustration 3A for further details on this critical technique, which cannot be omitted.

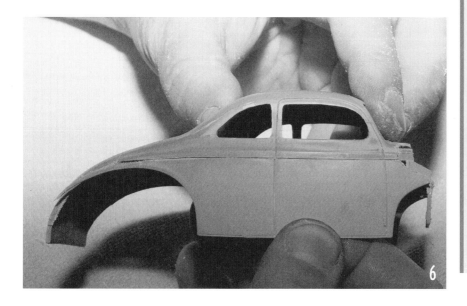

Quick Tip

It is crucial to remove the section from the body at its most vertical point. That is, don't take a slice from an angled portion of the body or you will have to narrow the body or widen the narrower part.

When sectioning a model with a strong horizontal character line (like a '49 Mercury), you will probably want to remove material from above and below the character line, depending upon how you want to proportion the upper extension of the wheel well to the top of the fender and hood.

7 Reattach the body temporarily to the fender unit to check out the reduction of height in the body. Note how important the body-sectioning technique has been to the design of the model, even though it is subtle.

8 Because the bottom of the hood will be so fragile when separated from the top of the hood, make your first cut below the tape line, followed by a slice on top of the tape line. Because of the strong radius of the hood, take great care to make your cuts square.

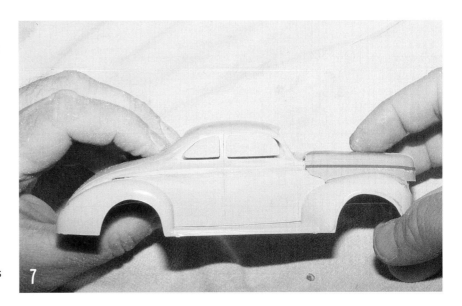

7

8

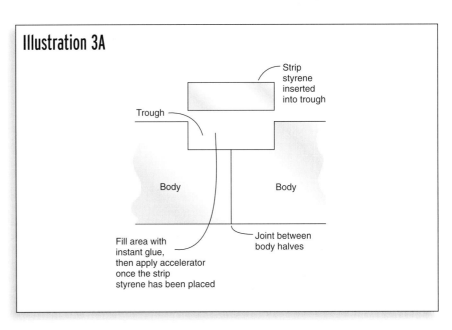

Illustration 3A

Strip styrene inserted into trough

Trough

Body

Body

Fill area with instant glue, then apply accelerator once the strip styrene has been placed

Joint between body halves

9 Rejoin the two hood sections using the techniques described earlier in this chapter. With the hood reattached to the body, note how the hood is now more slim and lithe, matching the body. Note here that the joint between the upper and lower body halves has been smoothed with some catalyzed polyester putty, and then sanded smooth with a coarse sanding stick. Next, a coat of primer is needed.

10 A coat of primer on the body makes plain the subtle, but significant, changes made to the body after the top chop and body sectioning, especially with the fenders temporarily in place.

11 After reducing the body in height, you must make a similar reduction in height in the interior. With the '40 Ford, it is easy to take out a slice from the top of the interior side panels. Then, tape the dash of your choice (either the kit piece or a dash imported from another kit) to the interior bucket and check out the fit.

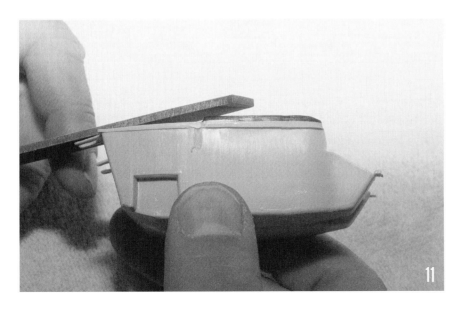

Chapter

four

Custom Fenders and Lights: Shed Some New Light!

Almost without exception, factory fender and lighting designs could use improvement. Often, production considerations (including the cost of a more graceful rendering of fender shapes and lighting) take precedence over good design. A good customizer understands that a lithe, flowing design can be achieved by the deft manipulation of the best elements of the factory design. One way to do this is by introducing sympathetic headlight and taillight shapes.

This section will first focus on reworking the venerable shape of the front fenders and hood of our '40 Ford. By flaring the front fenders upward, we can punctuate the new elliptical headlight shapes. Extending the length of the hood, and dropping it down between the fenders, we can avoid the prominent proboscis of the factory shape. The rear fenders, too, come in for their share of fairly aggressive work. They are molded to the body and fitted with some long taillights that mimic the diminishing width of the fenders as the eye moves toward the rear window.

Of course, there are other design possibilities. As you work through these photos, think of ways in which you could make your next custom model car project more graceful.

Left: 1940 Ford, '90s style. Right: 1940 Ford, '50s style. Both by Mark S. Gustavson

1 When viewed from the front, the front fenders of a '40 Ford are heavy. To complement the slightly elliptical shape of the headlights, let's remove some material from the fender just to the inside of each headlight. This alteration will relieve some of the heaviness of the fender. Check out the difference here: the passenger side has already been reshaped and features the new headlight that we will create.

2 The shaded pattern on the driver's front fender marks the area to be removed. Note how the shaded areas are on top of fender, at the apex of the curve, and just to the outside of the stock headlight shape.

3 Start by creating a trough that marks the deepest point of the area to be removed. Once you achieve the desired depth, you can start to remove material from adjacent areas to create a gentle ramping effect (see Illustration 4A).

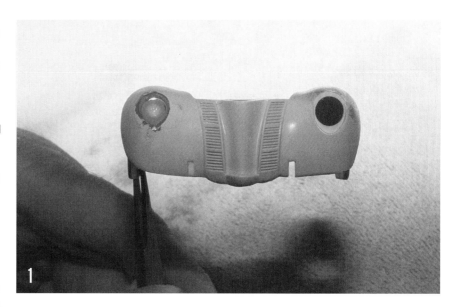

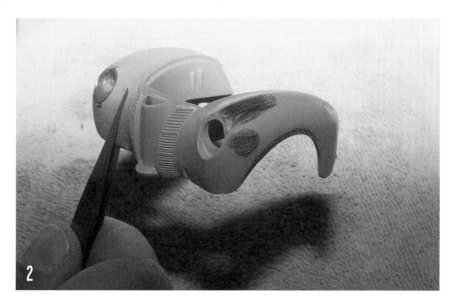

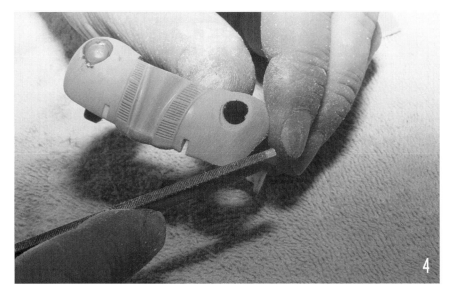

4 Part of our effort to customize the front fenders includes reshaping the outside radius of the front fender. In this case, the squarish lower outside edge of the fender is filed back to introduce a more graceful curve to the fender. Be careful not to remove too much material; start with a medium flat file, proceed with 220 paper, then proceed to 400 paper.

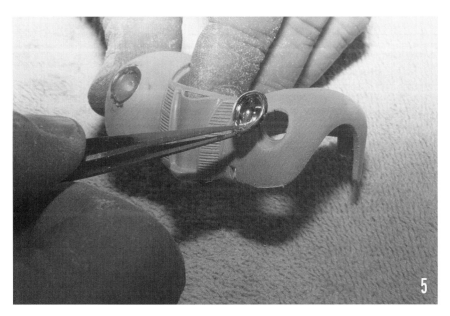

5 Now, let's do something with the awful stock '40 Ford headlight arrangement. In this case, an elliptical headlight shape will replace the original unit. Position the '37 Ford headlight bezels (from the Monogram kit) next to the fender to determine what changes have to be made to integrate the earlier bezel into this fender. The goal here is to have the outside dimensions of the bezel flow into the reshaped fenders.

Quick Tips

Think about making the shape of the headlight and taillight lenses part of the shape of the fender.

Try to make the headlight and taillight designs fit into the overall design of the fenders. Avoid jolting or disrupting designs, like sticking bullet taillights everywhere.

Remember to create enough room for wiring harness for the lights—practicality counts for a lot!

Protect chrome bezel plating by using House of Kolor Spray Mask. Avoid other masking products.

Illustration 4A

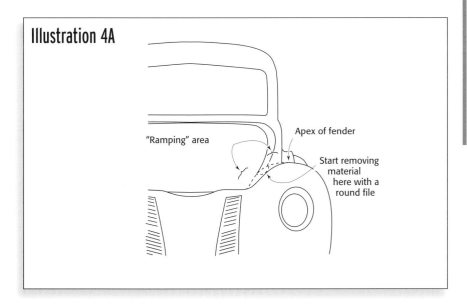

"Ramping" area

Apex of fender

Start removing material here with a round file

6 In this case, we'll have to remove the incut shape to the stock headlight opening and widen the opening For this application, it is best to use a round cutter in your motor tool and a moderate speed to remove the material. Constantly check and recheck the headlight bezel to the fender to be certain that you do not remove too much material.

7 After some careful and judicious cutting, the headlight bezel can be fitted to the fender. Note that the vertical center line through the headlight bezel (using the peak at the bottom of the bezel) is slightly canted toward the middle of the model.

8 Use a small bead of instant adhesive around the entire circumference of the bezel, and install the bezel on the fender. (Be certain that the inward cant of this headlight bezel matches the other side.) Use 600-grit paper to remove the chrome just from the outside of the bezel—this is necessary so that the putty can adhere to the bezel. Be extra careful to avoid damaging the chrome on the inside of the bezel. When the model is painted, the clear lens will be installed into the opening and the part will have to be reflective.

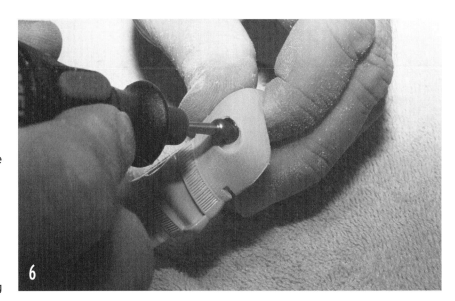

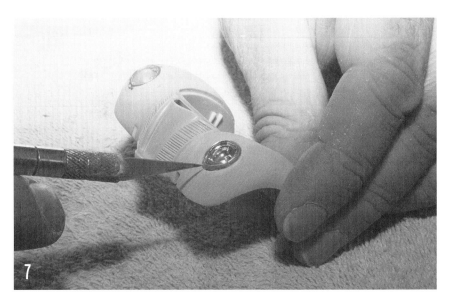

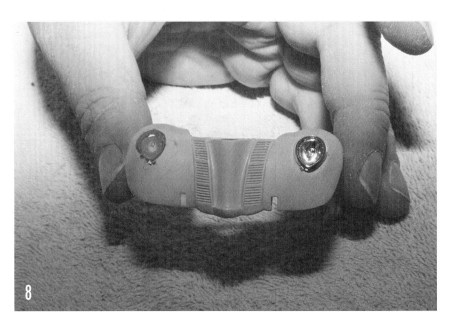

9 After positioning the lens and attaching it firmly, we must fill in the very slight gap between the outside of the bezel and the adjoining fender with some catalyzed spot putty. Again, be careful not to let the putty slip into the interior of the bezel.

10 Drip the Spray Mask into the bezel with the end of a paintbrush. Be careful not to let the mask slip outside of the bezel. (Note that the fenders are pointed straight up.) Two coats may be necessary. In a pinch, you can use fresh rubber cement, but that is a much less satisfactory material.

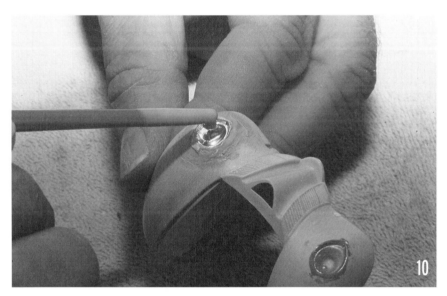

11 When the putty has set up, use some 220-grit sandpaper to initially shape the putty. Once again, be extremely careful not to damage the inside of the bezel. When you prime the fender, you'll have to mask the bezel. In this photo, both headlight bezels have been masked with Spray Mask.

Masking Chrome

At this stage (but probably not before), it is wise to protect the chrome on the interior of the bezel by masking it. I like House of Kolor brand Spray Mask, which is a water-soluble latex rubber product. It is infinitely superior to any competitive product.

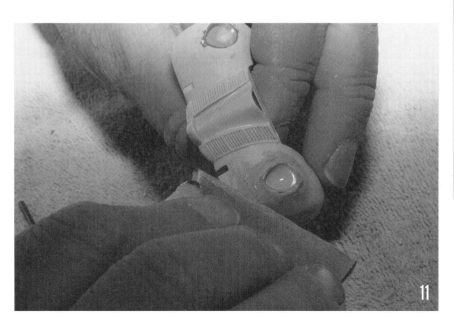

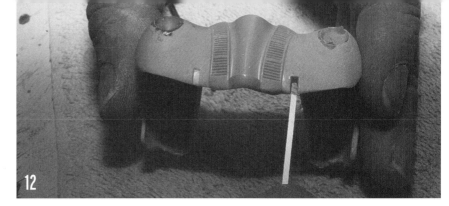

12 Let's fill the stock front bumper bracket holes. Cut some strip styrene of appropriate width. After lining the fender opening with a bit of instant glue, place the tip of some of the strip styrene on the body and apply accelerator. When the adhesive has kicked, cut off the bottom with nippers or a hobby saw. If you have positioned the strip styrene carefully, some careful filing with an elliptically shaped hobby file may eliminate the need for putty.

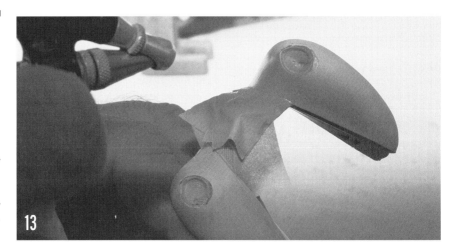

13 After lightly roughing up the entire area with a fine sanding stick, check out your work by applying some primer on one side. Since a final decision has not yet been made on the grille design, it has been masked off for the application of primer. During the body-work phase, it's a good idea to mask off all detail areas to prevent primer buildup.

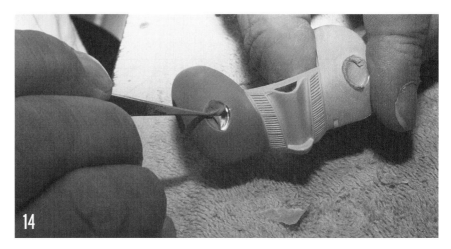

14 Using small tweezers, pull away the masking material to better envision the design. A hint: use the Spray Mask liberally so when you remove the masking periodically through the project it will be easier to do so without damaging the chrome. It is good to remove the spray masking from time to time during your work.

15 Attach your front fender assembly to the body. It is crucial that the body-to-fender interface is absolutely even and square. Once it was attached, we decided to remove some additional material from the inside of the front fenders so the headlight shape might be more emphasized and so the hood could rise more dramatically from the fender-headlight area. Mark the area first with a pencil.

16 Grab a round file and start to remove the material. Start at the center of the area to be removed; this is the deepest area and must be attacked first, since you can then taper the adjoining area upward onto the surrounding area.

17 Midway in the process, the area is somewhat rough with file marks from the file. Don't be concerned about the roughed-up area at this stage.

18 Roll some 220-grit paper (it comes in several different colors) into a curved shape and sand the area rough-shaped in the previous photo. Don't use a coarse sanding stick at this point because that won't produce a round shape. (The sandpaper, when bent, will maintain its curvature.) Follow with 360-grit, then 400-grit paper. Next, clean the area with your toothbrush, then wash thoroughly with warm water mixed with liquid dishwashing soap. Dry thoroughly.

19 Visit your paint booth again and apply a couple of medium coats of primer, letting the first coat flash off before applying the second coat. At this stage, it is important to check out the work done so far. When it's dry to the touch—usually 15 to 30 minutes, depending on your climate—take a look at the result. Check out the graceful curves that focus the eye on the elliptical headlights. At this point, for the sake of good workmanship, apply a thin coat of putty to the underside of the reworked fenders.

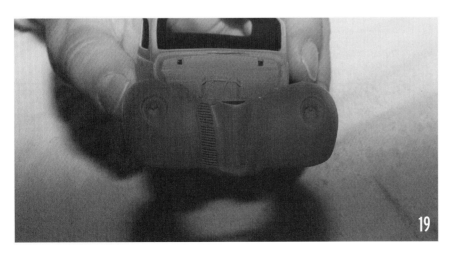

20 Let's start to do some grille work now. Grab your motor tool and start to grind away the stock grille work. Proceed carefully so that you don't grind through the fender.

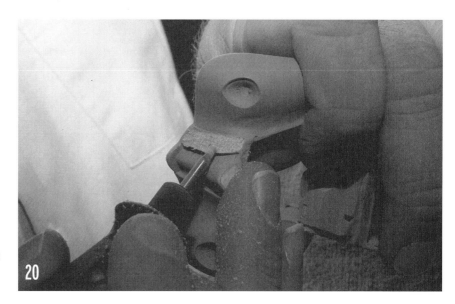

21 Though this effort has resulted in a very dramatic change to our project '40 Ford, there are even more radical changes in store.

22 It is important to interface the hood at this stage. Note how the sectioned hood nicely nestles down onto our revamped fenders. Note too how there is a much more dramatic sweep between the deepest part of the fender inside of the headlights and the upsweep of the hood. Between this step and the next, the hood has been dramatically dropped between the fenders, sitting atop a newly-formed grille. Note, too, how the hood line sweeps up to the base of the A pillar.

23

23 With a few coats of primer on the body, the substantial changes to the front end give our new-age '40 Ford custom almost a European appearance. We will insert a simple photoetched mesh grille in the opening.

24

24 Once the rear fender assembly has been separated from the running board (leave the side-to-side braces in place), employ your flat file to remove remnants of the kit's running board. Again, be careful not to remove any material from the shape of the fender.

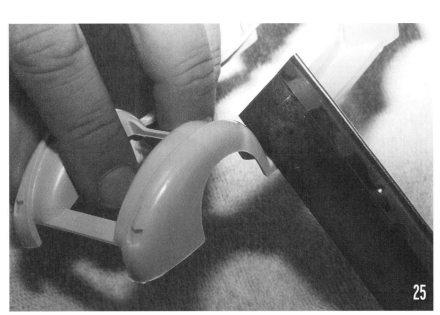

25

25 The best rear fender design can be accomplished by molding the fenders to the body. Using a fine-tooth hobby saw, make a cut line in front of the leading edge of the fender. Cut right through the running board, since you won't be using it anyway. Be careful not to cut into the fender itself.

26 Test-fit the rear fender assembly to the body. You will notice that there is a slight gap between the body and the inside of the fender.

27 Before we can fill that gap, we need to attach the fender assembly to the body. Rough up the mating surfaces (the interface between the fenders and the body) with a piece of 220-grit autobody paper. A moderate application of instant glue, aided by a spritz of accelerator, does the job.

28 Reinforce the inside of the body by applying a bead of instant glue around the fender-to-body interface. There is no substitute for a good, thorough bond.

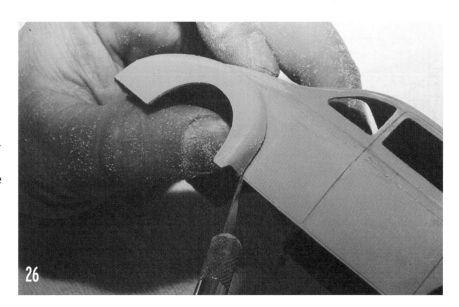

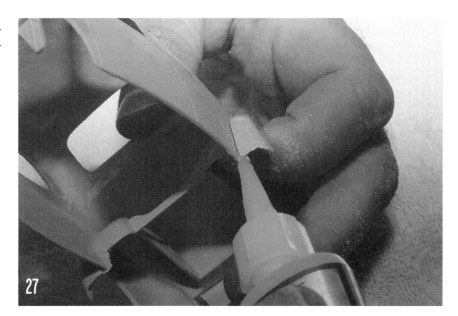

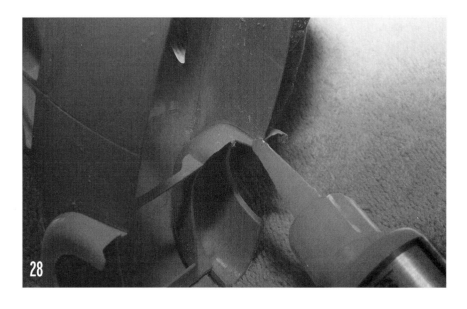

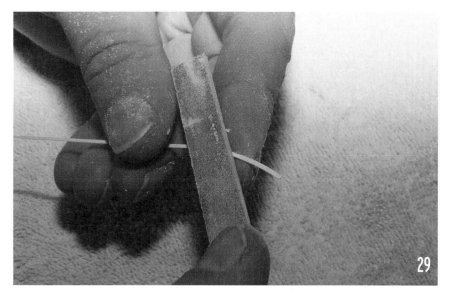

29 Now it is time to address the gap. The combination of a bit of shaped styrene strip and some instant glue will easily take care of this problem. Using a sanding stick, shape a piece of strip styrene roughly into a triangle.

30 Apply a moderate bead of instant glue into the gap between the inner fender shape and the body, and then press your shaped strip styrene into the gap around the entire circumference of the intersection. You will need an extra piece near the bottom of the rear of the fender since the gap is larger there. Don't worry if the strip styrene is longer than the gap to be filled; in fact, for ease of application, a longer-than-necessary strip keeps the adhesive off your hands. When the instant glue cures with a spritz of instant adhesive, just trim off the excess strip styrene.

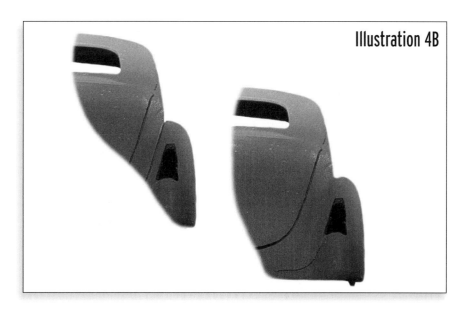

Illustration 4B

31 Shape the strip styrene you installed in the previous step. Grab a round hobby file and gently file the styrene into a gentle radius. Be careful, you don't want to remove too much material—not only does the strip styrene bridge an esthetic gap, but it strengthens the entire assembly. Just introduce a gentle transition between the fender and the body. See Illustration 4B (page 49).

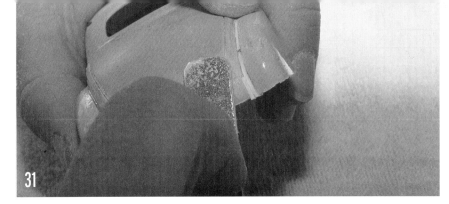

32 Once your file has roughly shaped the interface, you need to smooth it. Use a coarse or medium sanding stick, or a piece of 360 autobody paper. Remember that you want to do most of the bodywork in styrene before using putty. Repeat these steps for the other side, and be careful that both sides match. Now, apply a thin coating of putty, sand it when cured, and apply a thin coat of primer to check your work. If you have worked carefully, everything should be in good shape, needing only minimal further work.

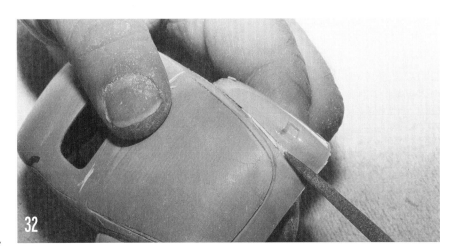

33 We need to flare out the rear wheel wells to permit the use of larger-than-factory tires. This technique really requires two steps. For now, let's pencil in a line that will roughly cover the entire circumference of the opening. You can remove the material in several ways; a round cutting head or, as here, a sanding drum on a motor tool. Don't use a flat file.

34 Rolling the extreme lower rear edge of the fender helps soften the shape and introduces a bit of gracefulness to the fender. Use a flat file, first, to remove the lower sharp corner. Follow up with a coarse, then a medium sanding stick over the lower edge of the fender to subtly roll the lower edge of the fender by eliminating the sharp, right-angle shape.

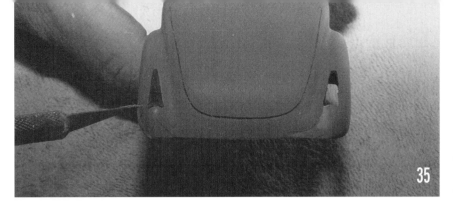

35 Let's create some custom taillights. Retrieve some scrap clear red taillight material from an old kit. A rectangular taillight, pointed toward the front of the model, would nicely mimic the shape of the fender. Make a pencil tracing to determine the shape, transfer it to the taillight material, and then cut out with a fine-tooth saw. Since there is a right and left to these lenses, make sure both sides match.

36 Drill a series of small holes in the fender, along the pencil line, with a pin vise, then remove the plastic with a hobby saw. Go slowly; don't remove too much. Test-fit the lenses; a fine sanding stick on the outside of the lenses and a flat hobby file on the inside of the fender cutouts will reconcile the two shapes. Here the lens is test-fitted on the driver's side and a character line has been introduced just below the opening, passing beneath the trunk. The lower edge of the trunk now is parallel to the character line. Subtle changes like this are as critical to good design as a major operation.

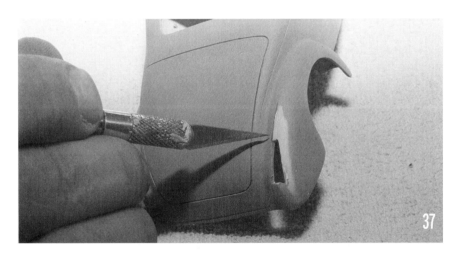

37 To further emphasize the taillight shape and to pull the eye of the viewer along the length of the fender, let's continue the character line forward and on the inside of the lenses. Again, create the incut shape with a flat hobby file. Depending on the application, you may also have to shape the taillight lens. Use progressively finer sandpaper, then finally plastic polish, on your lenses.

38 With the lenses shaped and test-fitted, evaluate the overall design. Notice the smoothly reshaped rear fenders, deck lid, taillight lens, and custom roof. The best parts of the Ford have been maintained, while the clunky elements have been eliminated. This is the essence of good customizing.

five

Brighten Up Your Model: How to Create Chrome Moldings

Whether you are building a custom vehicle or a version of a factory car that was never offered in a kit, you will undoubtedly be faced with the prospect of creating new side trim for your model. Only rarely will original factory side trim be acceptable for your new custom.

As with every other customizing task, there really isn't much to accomplishing these tasks once you become acquainted with the techniques and tricks. The side trim procedure specified below requires that you have previously completed, shaped, rough-sanded, primed, sanded, and reprimed the area to be fitted with trim to next-to-paint stage. You cannot do any bodywork in the affected area after installing the trim.

Dan Thomas's replica of the Hirohata Mercury

1 Though it is not widely known, you can attach strip styrene over lacquer primer if you follow a few simple steps. First, rough up the surface with 600-grit sandpaper or a fine sanding stick.

2 Using a graphite pencil (never a marker pen), draw the desired shape onto the panel. If you don't like the shape, or if you make a mistake, simply erase the line or use 600-grit sandpaper to remove the lines. Trace the shape onto a file card (either the inside or outside of the shape), and then transfer that tracing to the other side, using the same baseline to locate the tracing.

Quick Tips

Don't leave squared-off ends of strip styrene at the termination of your custom-built chrome moldings. Think about shaping them to fit the shape of an adjacent belt line or other body shape.

You can create a double-level molding by combining flat styrene with a strip laid on edge. See Illustration 5A

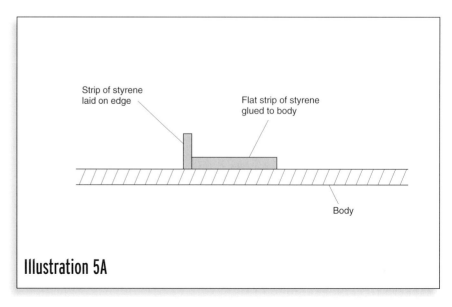

Strip of styrene laid on edge

Flat strip of styrene glued to body

Body

Illustration 5A

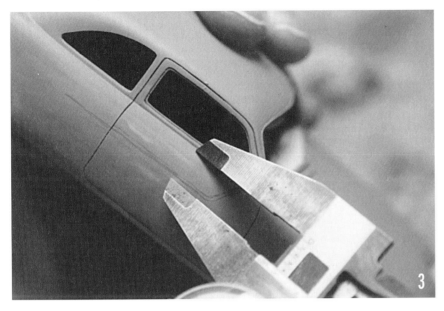

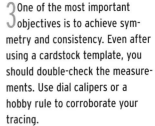

3 One of the most important objectives is to achieve symmetry and consistency. Even after using a cardstock template, you should double-check the measurements. Use dial calipers or a hobby rule to corroborate your tracing.

4 You can select almost any shape of strip styrene, but here a strip of .040 styrene is used. It is best to thin the strip styrene before you use it in order to make the application easier and more precise. Simply run a modest amount of liquid solvent (I like Testors) along the side that will be placed on the model. This will make the styrene easier to bend. Wait about 20 seconds.

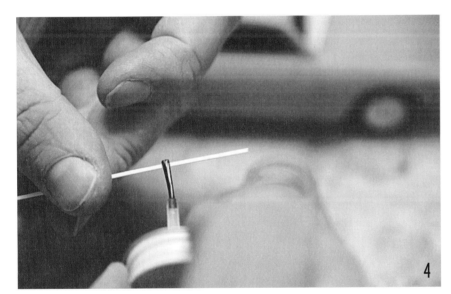

5 Now, apply another bit of liquid solvent on the side of the trim that will be pressed to the surface, and attach the strip styrene above or below your scribed line. In this application, it is placed just above the line. Make sure you do the same on both sides. Continue to lay the piece along your scribed line, and then press it down gently.

6 While things are still a bit mobile, recheck your work with the calipers; often, the styrene strip will wander or your scribed line may be obscured. Check and recheck your work every step of the way. Wait for about 10 minutes while the liquid solvent penetrates the surface and affixes the part to the body. Be patient.

7 Roughly estimate how much styrene you will need to bend upward to meet the beltline. Overestimate the amount of material, obviously. Use a pair of cutters rather than pressing the styrene to the body and then cutting it with a hobby blade—you don't want to mar the surface.

8 Again, soften up the strip styrene by laying a quick coating of liquid solvent along the length to be bent. Wait 20 to 30 seconds before proceeding.

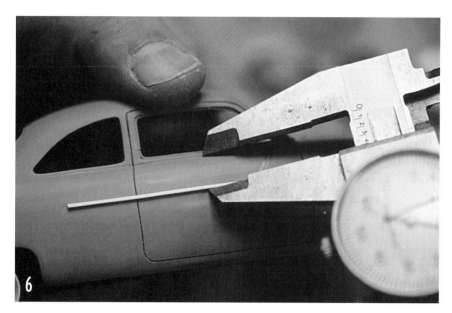

9 Using a pair of sharp-tipped tweezers, gently bend the plastic to conform to your traced line. Work slowly here. You don't want to fracture the strip styrene, thereby interrupting a smooth radius of the styrene as it moves upward toward the beltline.

10 Bend the shape so that it mates up with the belt line. Then, while holding the styrene strip place with your tweezers, apply a bit of liquid solvent to the underside of the strip and press it to the body. Once most of the bend is attached to the body, use your hobby blade and trim the upper extension of the strip styrene to mate with the belt line. (It will at one angle or other, depending upon your application.) Apply just a tiny bit of solvent to the underside of the uppermost extension of the styrene and press it to the body.

11 Wait 30 minutes before applying additional solvent, checking the entire time to make sure that the whole length has adhered flush to the body. Be patient. Now apply a very modest amount of solvent to the interface between the trim and the body to seal the edge. Set the model aside for at least 12 hours. Once the solvent has completely evaporated, it is time to shape the trim. Remember, real trim is not composed of hard right-angle shapes. Here, a slight crown is being shaped: a file is used to insure uniformity, but be careful not to nick your bodywork with it.

12 Rather than just letting the trailing edge of the trim end in a right angle to the length of the body, let's trim it at an angle to meet the angle of the C pillar. Just trim the length with a hobby blade, being exquisitely careful not to mar the surrounding primed bodywork.

13 Also, don't forget to create a small cut line whenever your new custom trim crosses a panel line. Details like this are essential. Think about what you are doing.

14 It is also important to run your hobby knife along the interface between the body and the trim to clean up any spurs or other surface irregularities.

15 Bend a piece of 600-grit autobody paper to a sharp line and run the paper around the interface between the base of the trim and the surrounding body. This will clean up any surface irregularities, thereby giving you a clean, sharp line that will make easier the later application of a foil product.

16 After painting, use standard procedures to attach your Bare Metal Foil. In this case, the result can be impressive.

six

Open Up Your Doors and Other Hinged Panels

One of the crowning achievements for model car builders is the construction of operational panels on a model. If it's done well, little else can add the sense of realism and sophistication that an opening door, trunk, hood, or other panel can achieve. However, probably no other operational feature of a model is so commonly botched. Too many modelers try to transplant plastic hinges from kits with operating doors, or they fail to install bodywork between the interior and the body (for instance, that seen when the doors are opened).

Vince LoBosco's '51 Chevy

The fact of the matter is that reliable, strong hinges that will operate realistically must be crafted from metal, whether you use the ancient paper-clip technique or make the more contemporary and realistic mechanically shaped brass hinges using materials from Special Shapes company (available in many hobby stores).

The model featured here is my Dream Truck[2]. Even after the substantial stress caused by stripping off the old paint and modestly restyling the model, the hinges still work perfectly. And nearly eight years after my Mercari was constructed, I can still literally slam those doors shut. There is no substitute for strong, soldered brass hinges.

1 The first thing to do is to construct the pivot point for the hinge. I used the solid rectangular brass stock from Special Shapes company (available from a good hobby shop). Make four and be sure they all match. Notice that the apex of the curve does not extend to the lowermost extension of the long arm. See Illustrations 6A and 6B for details.

2 Acquire some .080 tubing (I used copper tubing) and solder the hinges to the tubing. The hinge arms should sit flat on the workbench after they are soldered to the tubing. Use some flux on the tubing first to ease soldering. Apply the tip to the assembly long enough to get a good soldering joint—it will flow out and have a bright appearance when cooled—but not so much as to loosen the adjoining solder joint. An easy way to avoid that problem is to tape down the tube and the hinge before doing the second hinge. If you have worked carefully, only minimal cleanup will be necessary with a round file. (Be sure not to loosen the joint by removing too much of the solder.)

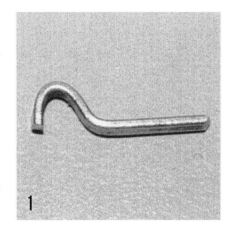

Quick Tips

Build your hinges and glue them in place with the door panel flush with the adjacent panels. A smooth transition between stationary and moving panels is essential.

Bevel the inside of the moving panel adjacent to the hinge to prevent the operational panel from binding.

Make your hinges from metal.

You should fashion some sort of latch to keep the operating panel closed. Check out Illustration 6A.

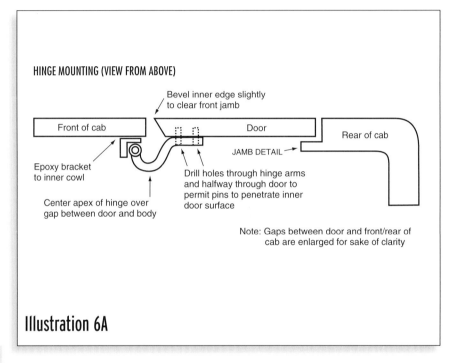

HINGE MOUNTING (VIEW FROM ABOVE)

Bevel inner edge slightly to clear front jamb

Front of cab

Door

Rear of cab

JAMB DETAIL

Epoxy bracket to inner cowl

Drill holes through hinge arms and halfway through door to permit pins to penetrate inner door surface

Center apex of hinge over gap between door and body

Note: Gaps between door and front/rear of cab are enlarged for sake of clarity

Illustration 6A

Illustration 6B

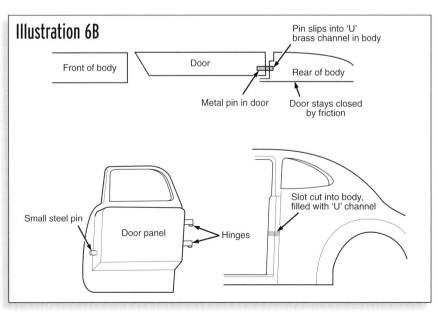

Pin slips into 'U' brass channel in body

Front of body

Door

Rear of body

Metal pin in door

Door stays closed by friction

Slot cut into body, filled with 'U' channel

Small steel pin

Door panel

Hinges

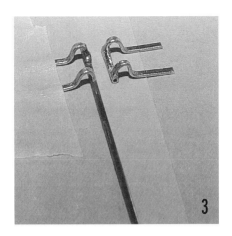

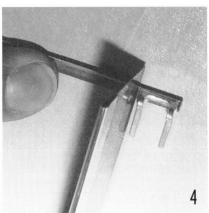

3 Now repeat steps one and two and make up two identical hinge arm assemblies. It is essential that the radius of the pivot and the dimensions of the parts be identical in all the assemblies.

4 Once both hinges have been soldered to the tube, then you will need to trim off the tubing on the outside of the hinge assembly. Use a fine-tooth hobby saw and proceed carefully. You are just trying to remove any excess material to the outside of either pivot arm.

5 Once you have established the width of the hinge assembly, you must build a receiver for the hinge. I choose a right-angle piece of brass .120 by .120, with .015 wall thickness, from Special Shapes. Solder a small bit of .015 flat brass to one end and trim and file it so that it matches the right-angle shape. Once the solder has cooled, place the hinge assembly in the receiver to determine the width of the receiver.

6 Pushing the pivot assembly up against one end of the pivot assembly, use a hobby saw to cut off the right-angle receiver. Make sure that your cut is square.

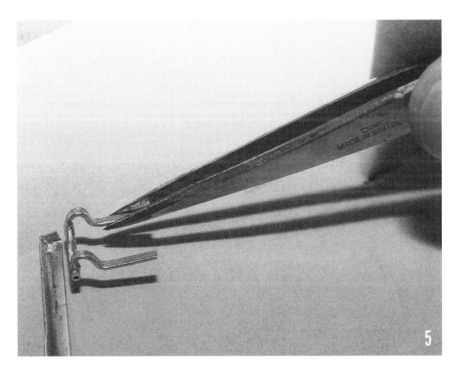

7 Once you have cut off the end of the receiver, it is time to solder a piece of .015 brass to the receiver in order to contain the hinge and keep it from wiggling. Tape down a piece of flat brass, tin it with flux, and tin the receiver with flux. Using tweezers to hold the receiver to the flat brass sheet (and to protect your fingers from the heat), solder the parts together. It is not important to get the receiver square to the small piece of flat brass, since you will be trimming the brass sheet.

8 Hold the completed receiver with tweezers and trim the base with a fine-tooth hobby saw. You don't have to cut the flat brass to shape before you solder it, since you can always cut away the excess and finish up with a flat hobby file.

9 Here you can see the operation of the hinge. The hinge assembly needs a bit more careful filing so that the length of the pivot tube does not extend beyond the pivot arms.

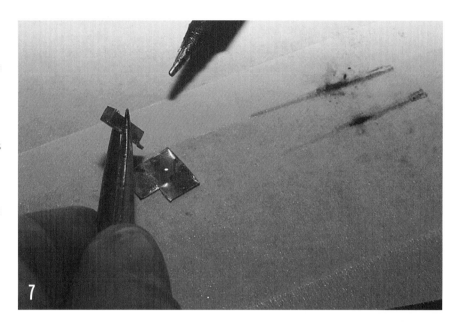

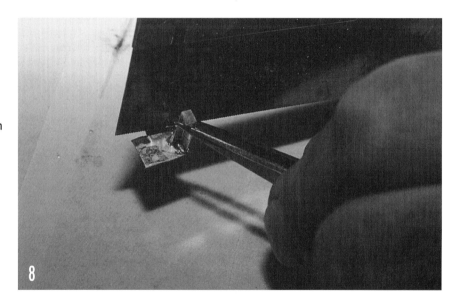

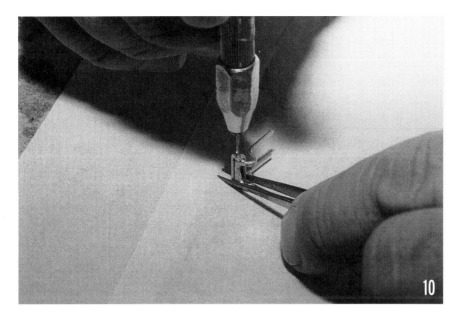

10 You'll have to drill a .030 hole through either end of the flat pieces (sitting at right angles to the length of the receiver) that will pass through the tube to which you soldered the hinge arms. The pivot assembly must be held tightly to the receiver. Then, when you drill the hole and install a pivot shaft, the pivot assembly will rotate tightly in the receiver. It is essential to make sure that the holes in either end of the receiver match with the tube. Careful measuring and some astute "eyeball engineering" are critical here.

11 Each hinge assembly is composed, left to right, of the receiver assembly, the .030 brass pivot arm, and the pivot assembly. Make sure that the assemblies for both doors match. The brass wire should be just slightly longer than the receiver. The pin should have one splayed end to prevent it from pulling through the entire assembly. Insert the pin through the receiver, into the pivot arm assembly, and out the other end through the receiver. Using only two-part epoxy, deposit a small drop on both outside fascias of the receiver to retain the pin.

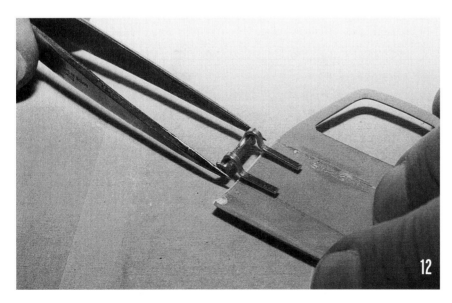

12 Since these doors will open outward from the body, rather than inward toward the jamb, as on modern vehicles, the hinge will mount this way on the body. It is important to mount the hinges in a particular way, which can't be successfully shown in a photo. Therefore, please refer to Illustration 6C. Install the hinges permanently once you have fashioned the critical interior components and fitted them to the model. They will include the dash, interior door panels, dome light, seat assembly, gas/brake/clutch assemblies, a console, and so forth, depending upon your design.

13 Seen from the outside of the model, this placement of the hinge will allow the door to swing out and away from the cowl.

14 You will need to create a stop around the door opening on the body, against which you could lay a small-diameter black wire to simulate weather stripping once the body is painted and rubbed out. This assembly will also give the door something to push up against when it is closed; this will keep the upper door frame from going too far in.

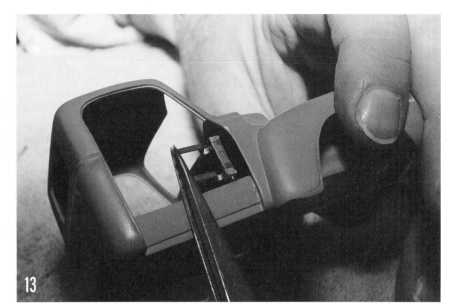

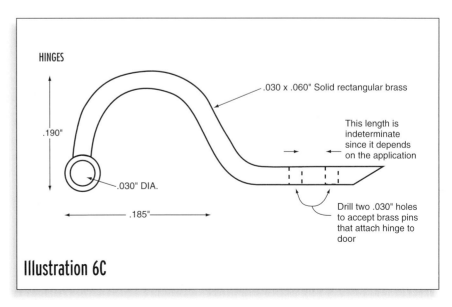

HINGES

.030 x .060" Solid rectangular brass

.190"

This length is indeterminate since it depends on the application

.030" DIA.

.185"

Drill two .030" holes to accept brass pins that attach hinge to door

Illustration 6C

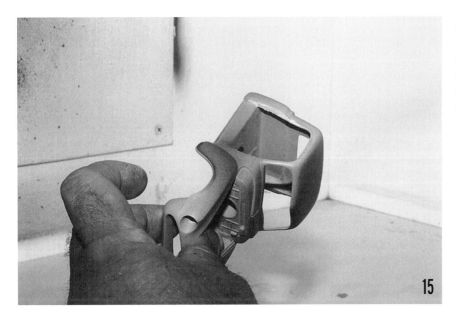

15 Of course, you also need to create the body side of the door jamb to achieve a realistic appearance. Make this part out of styrene strip and attach with instant adhesive.

16 Depending upon your design, you will also need to create a deep floorboard jamb, once again, for a realistic appearance.

17 You will have to thin out the edges of the door to achieve a more realistic appearance. Before you add an structural detail, use a round or elliptical file to consistently reduce the thickness of the panel just near the edge of the panel. Don't try to reduce the thickness throughout the entire panel. You are only trying to create the illusion of scale thickness, and a uniformly thin panel would be quite weak (another reason to make parts from brass sheet).

18 The door also must have structural elements added to the inside so that the mounting location of the door panel can be fixed. The lower horizontal shape here is just higher than the elevation of the floor pan. Note here that the body and the floorboard have been jointed together so that the body can be strong and rigid. If you have planned your work carefully, the interior parts have been prefitted, which will mean that final assembly should not be difficult.

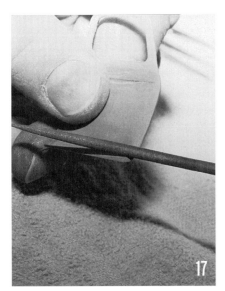

seven

Practical Construction and Assembly Considerations

After all of the bodywork has been completed, there are two remaining challenges to the custom model car builder. One of the greatest obstacles to custom model car construction is the matter of engineering how all of the elements go together cohesively in such a way that, if full scale, the vehicle could accommodate an actual human being and be operated on a public road. For instance, sectioning a model will change how the driver and passenger sit in the vehicle—is there enough height between the floor and the top of the bottom seat cushion so that the driver can operate the vehicle without fatigue? In another example, if a roof has been chopped or reshaped, can a driver and passenger see out of the windows so that the vehicle can be operated safely? Almost worse is a model that, if real, couldn't be driven on a city street because there isn't any wheel travel, or whose front wheels won't steer because no room has been left for that operation. The days of silly customs are over. This is the time for realistic custom vehicles in any scale.

The second greatest challenge is for the hobbyist to assemble the model so that all of the parts fit together—so that the model can be assembled after painting, with each part fitting to every

1965 Chevrolet by Bill Taylor

other part. The complexity of custom model cars is many times greater than that of a kit assembled essentially out of the box; in the latter case, you are relying chiefly upon the engineering decisions of the kit maker. When you build a custom model car, you have upset many if not most of the engineering and assembly considerations that are present in the real car and in the kit. If you have chopped the top on a model, or extended a fender, or sectioned the body, or even changed headlights and taillights, those actions affect other design and engineering elements of the model. In short, the custom model car builder faces the significant task of redesigning and reengineering the various elements of the model so that it not only goes together to produce a satisfying model, but is an intelligent model. If built full-scale, it would satisfy the twin considerations of good design and comfortable, realistic operation.

As with other custom model car objectives, the goal of designing and assembling an intelligent custom model car can be easily managed if you keep a few things in mind. Let's take a careful look at assembly and model design issues.

Rethink how to assemble a model. It is essential to rethink the ways to construct models. We have all been seduced by the kit-assembly procedures established more than 30 years ago that permitted kit manufacturers to quickly assemble promotional models for the major auto manufacturers. Those production considerations spilled over, of course, to the kits. They set the standards that, with only a few exceptions, have determined the way that hundreds of thousands of model builders have constructed millions of scale model vehicles. Think about it: you have a body, an interior "tub," a chassis, and underbody mated into one unit, and press-on bumpers and wheels. While it was fairly easy to combine those unrealistically assembled parts together and get a relatively decent result, the result was hardly realistic. How is that assembly procedure authentic, and does it actually assist

the hobbyist to construct a realistic custom model car? The truth of the matter is that it wasn't and didn't: no real car is assembled in the way that the model manufacturers have presented their kits. Until recently, most model car builders have either failed to recognize that fact or have chosen to ignore it and stick with the status quo. Only recently have major kit manufacturers like Revell/Monogram, AMT and Lindberg/Testors seen the light on this issue and begun to create separate interior panels, and provide separate frames with their kits.

Taking the cue from the kit manufacturers, but moving on to do a better job, what can you do to build a realistic custom model car? Here are a few suggestions.

Try to assemble the model in the way that a real car is assembled. This seemingly radical approach to design, construction, and final assembly is actually relatively easy. The auto manufacturers build their cars the way they do because they are faced with the same problems of uniformity, ease of assembly, and related matters that trouble thoughtful model car builders. The first thing to do, obviously, is to complete all of your customizing tasks first. Finish off the bodywork to the next-paint stage so that further work can rely upon an established body configuration. The next thing to do is to determine if you are going to build a body-on-frame model or a unibody model.

Unibody construction. If your model or design is of a unibody car, construct the underbody platform (either by modifying the kit piece or by scratchbuilding one). If you are going to open the doors, hood, and trunk, or otherwise modify the body or smooth out the inside of the roof (to remove ejection pins and so on), complete these tasks first. In fact, complete every significant task that would require you to have full access to the inside of the body cavity. For instance, you should smooth the underside of the roof and body panels if your customizing operation has affected those body components. Next, build all the hinge parts for your door, hood, and trunk

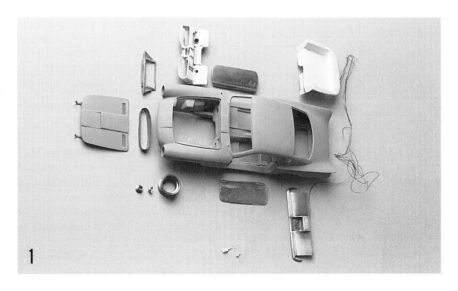

1 A current project of mine—the replica of a "lost" Lincoln-Mercury dream car from 1963—features unibody construction. All major components have been prefitted repeatedly to make sure they fit accurately so that their final installation is trouble-free. Note that the floorboards have been bonded to the body.

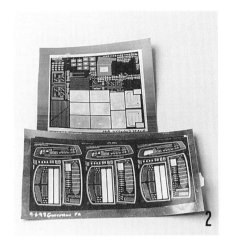

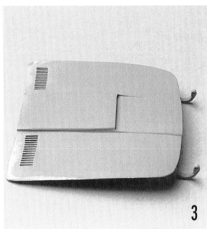

2 Many essential details—from ribbed floorboards to structural angles to exterior "chrome" window moldings—can be custom-made from photoetching. These items, created by Bob Wick and Fred Hultberg, are replicas of the various parts originally found on the Lincoln-Mercury dream car project, the Lynx.

3 Note here that hinges have been soldered to the scratchbuilt hood for the Lynx (hammered from brass in this example). A receiver assembly (see Chapter Six) was scratchbuilt and is attached under the front panel that stretches between the front headlights and above the grille. The louvers were actually photoetched pieces, custom-produced for this project by Bob Wick and Fred Hultberg, which I soldered to the rest of the scratchbuilt brass hood.

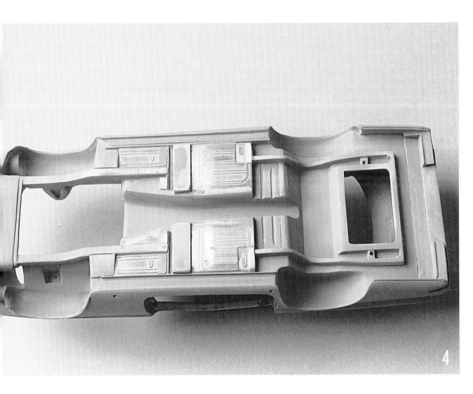

4 The floorboard on every uni-body car has stress ribs and other shapes to help eliminate the flex and strumming of the sheet metal, and to help strengthen the panel. These shapes can either be fashioned from strip styrene or, as here, they can be custom-photoetched on .006 brass.

hinges and then fit those parts to the body so that, when the model is painted and rubbed out, you can assemble the prefitted opening panels. This procedure will allow you to stabilize a body that has been weakened by opening up the doors, hood, and trunk.

Next, fashion all the mechanical elements so that you can test-fit the complete drive train and suspension. You should test-fit these components now and make whatever changes might be necessary to the unibody, including suspension pickup points, and then mate the unibody to the body shell.

Of course, final assembly of all of the interior and mechanical components will have to be accomplished by reaching in through the opened doors, trunk, and hood. However, if you have prefitted everything to the basic unibody, then everything should really click into place.

Body-on-frame construction. If your model is a body-on-frame type of construction, then you will have to create a floorboard and a separate frame. This can be tedious work, but the final reward is substantial. For instance, you can take two floorboard-chassis pieces from, for example, the AMT '49 Ford kit and cut the floor out of one and the frame out of the other. Or just scratchbuild a new underbody from sheet plastic or brass materials, using the kit part as a rough guide.

You will also need to create a frame onto which you can drop the body. That can be accomplished in a couple of ways. First, once you have removed the old floorboard from the frame, you can just clean up the frame or take the frame to a jeweler and have it cast in brass. Or you could scratchbuild a frame from brass or plastic and then fit it to the body. No matter which way the frame is made,

5 In this example, I separated the stock 1949 AMT kit frame from the floorboard to which it was molded. Then it was cast in brass. This chassis will be attached to the body by a series of small brass pins soldered to the frame "outriggers" and thence into corresponding holes in the body. In that way, the body will mount to the frame in the same way every time, both during the test and construction stage and during final assembly. This chassis will fit under a sectioned, shortened, and full-custom 1949 Ford that is being constructed as a tribute to the famed Valley Custom Shop.

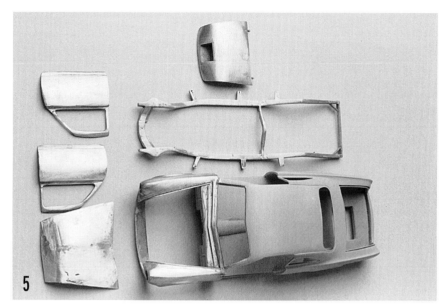

6 For the reconstructed Dream Truck[2], a Revell '64 Apache truck frame has been shortened and widened and is in the process of being fitted with the front suspension from a '56 Nomad. The heavily modified frame, here being test-fitted underneath my restyled Dream Truck[2] (once the featured model in the Custom Clinic articles in *Car Modeler* magazine) is reconciled here with a paper pattern for the photoetched floorboard ribbing. The model is being rebuilt and modestly restyled to correct many of the styling errors in the first version.

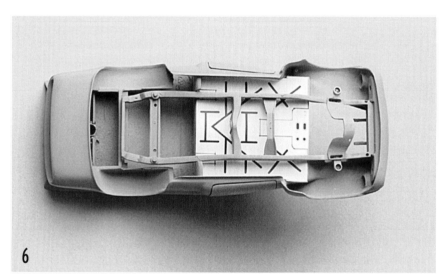

you have actually simplified your final construction tasks and provided a fresh canvas on which to apply your detailing tricks. The frame (and everything that attaches to it) is now a separate frame—a model in itself—to which you can attach all of the mechanical components. You can then fit that major assembly of subcomponents in turn to the body once you have painted and assembled the body.

Think about the compounding effect of tolerance drift. When you get a lot of parts that are supposed to go together, the combined physical intervals between those parts compound to the point that a little misfit in one area often results in a significant misfit in an adjacent area. You need to think about ways to reduce these tolerances.

Interface all parts. You will need to locate each part in relation to every other part. This consideration should also lead you to start to think seriously about how the dimensions of major subcomponents will influence the use and placement of other subcomponents. Use a locating pin approach to install major components. You must repeatedly test-fit the subassemblies on your custom model car before completion to be certain that the parts fit in the same place each time. Therefore, install small brass pins in pieces to locate the various components, major and minor, in the same place.

Treat every part as a model in itself. Fashion each element of the model as if it could be entered in a contest without being combined with other parts. By treating each part, then each subassembly, as if it alone could determine the character and quality of the entire scale custom model car, you are more likely to make sure that the fit, finish, and realistic appearance are consistent and convincing throughout.

Fit components with other components, and then to the body. Start by fitting small pieces to other small

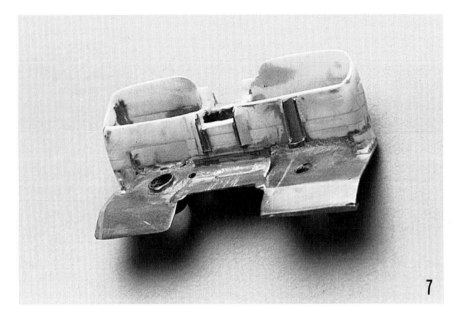

7 This dash assembly has been treated as a major subcomponent in my construction of the replica of the "lost" Lincoln-Mercury show car. It has been attached to a scratchbuilt firewall that snaps into the model, using the heater core access hole as the major locating point. Machined gauge bezels with photoreduced gauge faces will be fitted to this assembly. Then those parts will be fitted to a photoetched instrument fascia. Similarly, the instrument cluster fascia will host a machined bezel into which a vintage Ford clock will be fitted. Additionally, the pedal (brake and clutch) and throttle assemblies will be fitted to the brass firewall.

8 The entire dash-firewall assembly snaps into the body. The console, here in an early configuration, holds the dash into the model. Since other subcomponents have already been added to the dash-firewall and console, the impact of these parts on the rest of the body can be controlled during test-fitting and final assembly. This procedure makes it possible to include other equally complicated assemblies on the model.

pieces to create subcomponents, which you can in turn mate with other subcomponents to create major components. Fit major components with other components, then with the body, then to test for overall fit. It would be best to come up with a method to fit the pieces to each other uniformly so that you can best determine the actual ultimate configuration and fit before you paint.

Compound errors downward. By establishing the outer parameters of each subassembly and how they fit with other assemblies in the early stages of construction, you can work within the confines of those physical parameters and ensure correct fit of the entire subassembly in the model. This means that the dimensional errors (dimensional drift) will be contained within each subassembly and not compounded throughout the entire model. Again, test-fit parts repeatedly throughout the planning and construction phases and, in the process,

think about how to anticipate the effect that paint thickness will have on the fit of each part. Plan for the effect of paint thickness by very slightly increasing the space between the parts. The goal is to reduce the number and severity of the fit and finish problems that always crop up during final assembly.

Final considerations. Paint the exterior of the body early enough to allow you to determine whether there are any flaws, and to permit the paint to shrink before final polishing. Whether you're using lacquer or enamel, leave enough time (at least three weeks) for the paint to shrink, or "settle," before polishing. If you observe any paint or bodywork flaws early enough in the construction of your scale model car custom, then you can correct that problem and repaint the entire model. During this pre-final-assembly stage, you should fit all of the exterior panels and check the clearances between parts as they are operated.

9 Really small, complicated parts assemblies can also be treated as models in themselves and placed in another subassembly, which in turn is another subassembly for the overall model. In this case, a multipart Ford 4100-series 4-barrel carb (machined by Cody Grayland) will be carefully assembled and then fitted to the scratchbuilt 289 Ford K engine that I am constructing.

10 Research revealed that at least one of the six versions of the real "lost" Lincoln-Mercury dream car was fitted with Borraini wheels. Cody Grayland has created the rims (with the cross-lacing holes drilled), the hub, the nipples that will host the .009 stainless wire for the spokes, the knock-off hubs, and the two-part valve stems—all in 1/24 scale! After chrome-plating, the rims and hubs will be installed in the Plexiglas lacing fixtures so that the spokes can be correctly assembled. Each of these wheel assemblies will be a model in itself.

11 The front turn light for the Dream Truck[2], running light, and grille assembly for the body are machined so that the entire 13-part assembly can be held together by just slipping the parts together and then fitting the entire assembly to established set points—bosses—in the front grille opening on the reconstructed Dream Truck. Careful engineering, planning, and machining is necessary to create an assembly that will go together antiseptically. The rear grille work is identical to the front: reflective grids have been machined into the back side of the rear round red lens.

9

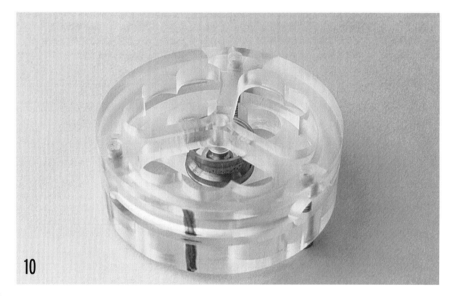

10

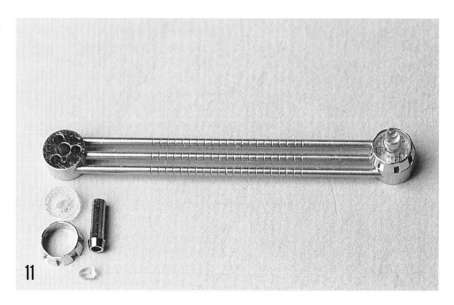

11

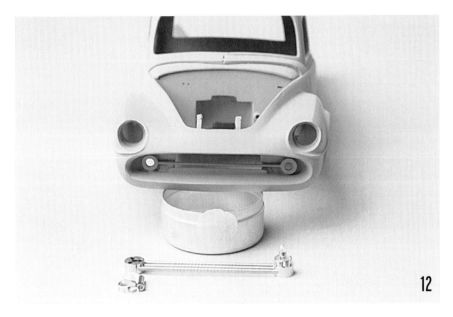

12 The entire assembly will fit into the points of contact in the front grille. The measurement between the center of each of the bosses is the exact center point of the grille work that will be slipped into the body. A bit of glue applied to the interface between the long chrome spears and the bosses in the body will hold the entire front grille assembly. The holes in the round grille bezel, behind the clear front lens, and the clear bullet tip that fits into the chrome spear permit the installation of small lightbulbs so front driving and turn lights can be fitted. The horizontal bars still need to be chrome-plated in this shot. Thanks to Steve Jansen for the chrome-plating.

13 In this assembly technique, the horizontal cross-bars fit into the round bezels without the need for glue; also, the entire bezel is assembled and located by the placement of the central chrome spear (on the tip of which is the turn light), which is the only part actually glued to the machined receptacle in the body. Final assembly should be a breeze because my design was magnificently translated into reality by Cody Grayland.

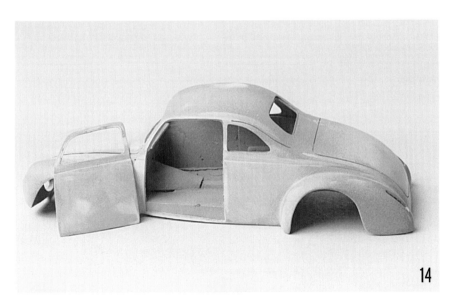

14 Even with a modest model, consider mating the body to the floor pan, and then dropping that assembly over the frame. In our feature model, the 1940 Ford coupe, we have installed the kit interior tub after cutting away the door panels to get the tub inside the customized body. The driver's door was cut loose and will be reinstalled after painting so that the interior can be positioned. It will take careful application of a thin strip of styrene around the perimeter of the door to compensate for the material removed when the door was cut out.

eight

Custom Body Preparation and Paint

Regardless of the level of customizing on a model, little is more important than the application of a sophisticated custom paint finish. Whether it's a candy finish, a pearl finish, or just a mile-deep solid finish, a flawless paint job is critical to the successful presentation of a scale model custom. There is an added challenge in getting a top-quality application on a custom model because the extensive bodywork requires extra work to prepare for paint. This chapter assumes that you will be using an airbrush to apply your paint; while not absolutely necessary to get a decent finish, an airbrush gives you the kind of control over paint thickness and application that is not possible with a spray can. For background information and an excellent general discussion of painting, I heartily recommend that you consult Pat Covert's excellent *Modeler's Guide to Scale Automotive Finishes,* available from Kalmbach.

While a full discussion of the intricacies of custom painting is beyond the scope of this book, let's walk through the body preparation and painting of our custom 1940 Ford. By following a handful of recommendations, and by using only top-of-the-line professional

Volkswagen by Don Fahrni

1 I highly recommend DuPont lacquer products for painting custom model cars, though almost all brands of lacquer primers, colors, and clear coat are excellent. The Fill 'N Sand (no. 131 S) product is an acrylic lacquer primer, while no. 30 S is a nitrocellulose product. Both products are excellent primers, though some modelers prefer 131 S. 30 S is somewhat darker than 131 S and, for that reason, can be used as a suitable guide coat. I recommend using an excellent grade lacquer thinner, selected to match the particular circumstances of your locale: there are different thinners for different weather conditions. Check with your paint jobber.

2 You cannot successfully apply lacquer colors over the top of primed bodywork; therefore, you need a sealer. One of the best sealers is DuPont's Variprime. Applied correctly in a mixture of 1 to 1, this sealer will successfully isolate the color and clear coats from the primer and bodywork. Allow the product to cure for at least 12 hours (preferably 24) before spraying on your first color coat. Be certain to use a two-canister, approved charcoal filter when using this catalyzed product. Read the Material Safety Data Sheets. *Safety is all-important.*

3&4 After you have applied a couple of coats of primer, let it dry thoroughly and then sand the model. Note that some high areas of the bodywork appear. Use a medium sanding stick at this stage. After this sanding, wash the model thoroughly, dry it thoroughly, and then apply another couple of coats of primer. The point here is to fill up the "valleys" and cut down the "mountains."

autobody products, anyone can achieve a lustrous finish that will rival the work of any full-size custom painter and do justice to your work. Here are some guidelines that you should read before you work through the accompanying photographs and captions:

• First, be careful to properly smooth the interface between the bodywork and the kit bodywork. This means that you should use a sanding stick or some kind of sanding block so that the panels are squared up with one another (see Illustration 8A). The last thing you want to do is to sand across a putty joint using only your fingers; you would accomplish little more than creating a trough or "valley" that would be the first thing seen by your audience. Sand across a surface and never sand along the putty joint.

• The second objective, closely related to the first, is to use a coarse enough paper to sand the putty and adjacent panels flat during the initial stages of your custom work. If, for instance, a custom model car builder were to start to sand a puttied joint with 400-grit paper, the puttied area would never make a smooth transition to the adjacent panels because the fine-grit sandpaper would just ride up and over the putty. Start with 220 autobody paper (used dry) to generally shape the area, then use a coarse sanding stick and finally a medium stick to finish the panels before applying the first coat of primer.

• The third objective is to do as much of the customizing work possible in the base materials (styrene, in most cases) rather than using putty to fill in mismatched, poorly executed, or incomplete work. And only use instant adhesive, with accelerator, to attach the basic parts together before applying putty. Solvent-based glues just soften the plastic, don't provide a dimensionally stable base for your work, and should be absolutely avoided.

• The fourth goal is to get all your body work finished (including all putty work) before applying any primer. Primer is intended to fill in very minor surface imperfections in preparation for paint and should not be used to detect moderate or significant bodywork flaws. If, after a coat of primer, you discover that an area needs a bit more putty, remove the primer on the area with a coarse sanding stick before applying more putty. Don't build up alternating coats of primer and putty that will simply cause problems when you apply the color and clear coats.

• The fifth goal is to avoid applying too much primer. Minimize primer coat film buildup by careful block-sanding to determine the suitability of the surface for paint. When more primer is needed, apply it only to the area that you have just worked over. (Mask other areas that will not be primed.) Be careful to avoid a heavy, thick application of primer and paint. Lacquer is particularly suited for this purpose because it is a thin painting system.

• The sixth goal is to use a single paint system throughout, unless you're a highly-experienced paint professional. That is, if you start using lacquer primer, it is generally best to stick with lacquer for color and clear

Thinning Lacquer Paint

25%	=	4 parts color or clear to 1 part thinner
33%	=	3 parts color or clear to 1 part thinner
50%	=	2 parts color or clear to 1 part thinner
100%	=	1 part color or clear to 1 part thinner
125%	=	4 parts color or clear to 1 part thinner
150%	=	2 parts color or clear to 1 part thinner
200%	=	1 part color or clear to 2 parts thinner
500%	=	1 part color or clear to 5 parts thinner

Lacquer Thinners
DuPont No. 3608 S Fast Dry
DuPont No. 3661 S Medium Dry
DuPont No. 3602S Slow Dry–High Gloss

Standard Thinning
Lacquer Colors	150%
Lacquer Clear	150–200%
Candies	150–300%
Final Clear	500% (used after color-sanding)

coats. Otherwise, you may encounter adhesion problems that could raise havoc with your project. Also, try to avoid mixing different brands of paint, even within a single painting system. Do not apply the products of different manufacturers over paints from other manufacturers except in the case of clear topcoats that appear to work over virtually any lacquer base colors. The exception to this is that you can mix pearl pastes (real) or faux pearl (mica-based) powders into any paint product.

• The seventh objective is to use a suitable sealer (preferably a catalyzed product) to encapsulate your body work from the chemically "hot" color and clear coats. Few things are more annoying than seeing "ghost" images (from bodywork, putty lines, or deleted scripts or chrome trim or bodywork) appear in the color and clear costs.

• The eighth goal, once you are near the painting stage, is to be sure to use sandpapers that are fine enough in order to avoid the appearance of scratches after your color and clear coats are applied. Like some enamels, lacquer is particularly sensitive to sanding scratches which are enlarged when color coats are applied. Before the final anticipated coat of primer, never use any paper coarser than 600 grit. Sand the concluding primer coat with 800 grit in preparation for the sealer. Once your sealer has thoroughly cured, sand it with 1200-grit paper. And use only autobody paper. The auto refinish industry has established universally-recognized sandpaper types that I use here. Never use household or woodworking sandpapers, which are graded differently and use harder grits than the autobody industry recommends. If you need to color-sand your top clear coats, get some genuine autobody 2000-grit sandpaper, and use it to carefully scuff the surface.

• The ninth objective is to use only regular autobody polishing products to rub down your paint job once the top clear coats have thoroughly cured (for at least two weeks). At all costs, avoid products that contain silicon or carnauba, including all floor wax products, some auto waxes, and the popular polishing kits. You can't paint over those products without using sophisticated products to remove those chemicals; additionally, those products tend to seal in the paint, which prevents it from "breathing" as it ages. I heartily recommend the Meguiar's brand products, starting with M-3 for initial polishing right after color sanding, and progressing to M-7 to remove swirls and other evidence of M-3. Use autobody products throughout your entire project!

• Finally, use a suitable air filtration system at all times. Putty dust, sanding residue, volatile organic compounds in lacquer, isocyanates in some catalyzed urethanes, and other chemicals common to all painting systems won't just make you feel crummy, they can kill you, often quickly. Buy protection and use it!

Of course, another big issue is how to mix the lacquer thinners and lacquer colors for correct application. Please consult the chart (page 79) for mixing formulas.

Note: Air brushes have small outlets, requiring thinner materials; therefore, always test-spray to achieve a smooth flow of material. Remember, there is an inverse relationship between coverage and the thickness of the paint: the thinner the paint, the better the flow. But better coverage is achieved with thicker materials, which are difficult to spray. Practice on several spare bodies with lacquer paint before progressing to a favorite project model.

Finally, you should become familiar with some of the terminology of professional painting. It will allow you to understand this text and converse with your paint jobber.

Base-coat/clear-coat system (B/C, as it is known in the industry) involves the application of a couple of coats of clear paint over a so-called high-solid base color, which is applied in turn over a primer/sealer. The high-solid base color used in this system is usually a metallic color, though many so-called solid colors can be applied in the B/C system as long as the solid color is specially mixed to accept the clear top coat. Most auto manufacturers use this system because it permits the overall paint film to be held to a minimum while ensuring a rich, lustrous finish (because of the clear). Typically, this system would be applied like this: primer/sealer, high-solid color coat, clear top coat.

Tri-coat system (T/C, as it is known in the industry) involves the application of a couple of coats of clear paint over a so-called glamour tint coat (usually involving the new mica pearl powders, sometimes mixed in a colored toner). The glamour tint coat is in turn applied over high-solid base color (in a color matching the tint coat), which is, of course, applied over the primer/sealer. Typically, this system would be applied as follows: primer/sealer, white high-solid underbase, white (mica) pearl, clear top coat. The system is used sometimes by

auto manufacturers on upper-line cars; the decade-old Cadillac Allante used this system when the pearl white was applied. This tri-coat system depends upon the uniform application of the color coat.

Single-stage system is nothing more than a solid or metallic color applied over a primer/sealer. No clear paint is necessarily involved in this system. Because the color must be color-sanded with 2000-grit 3M paper (used wet) to remove small flaws, it is usually best to use only solid colors. Sanding a metallic single-stage color almost always results in splotches in the color because some of the metallic paint is removed during the color-sanding step.

High-solid paint is a color specially mixed that increases the concentration of paint pigments mixed in with clear binders and other chemical ingredients. This color usually requires only a coat or two for full coverage. It is specially formulated to adhere to the underlying primer/sealer and to adhere also to the clear top coats. A high-solid color is a technical term; the paint cannot be created except by an experienced paint technician.

Clear-coat paint is the clear protective coating applied in a base coat/clear coat or tri-coat system. The clear coat can be an acrylic lacquer, enamel, or a urethane. Like the high-solid paint, clear paint must also be specially mixed with appropriate binders and other chemical ingredients to attach to the underlying high-solid color or the glamour tint coat. An appropriately mixed clear coat can be applied over a solid base color, but the solid base color (usually mixed in a high-solid format) must include special binders and other chemical elements to promote adhesion.

Primer/sealer is a term, sometimes used generically, to denote the coating that seals the underlying surface (in our case, styrene, resin, brass, or similar materials) and provides a uniform basis over which paint can be applied. Occasionally, a good coat of acrylic lacquer primer (DuPont's 30 S or 131 S are good choices) is adequate, though more often a coat of DuPont's Variprime (no. 615S) with Variprime Fast Converter (no. 620S) is necessary if bodywork has been done. Also, styrene tinted red, yellow, or green typically needs a sealer.

Color sanding means using very fine 2000-grit sandpaper with tepid water mixed with a drop or two of liquid soap. (Check to be sure that the liquid soap doesn't contain any silicone components.) The soap helps suspend in water the microscopic bits of paint that are actually removed during the sanding process. Sand the surface very lightly with this fine paper to remove the small dots of dust that invariably appear in the paint. You should sand only solid colors (in single-stage painting systems) or clear coats (in base coat/tri-coat systems). Take great care to avoid cutting through the solid color or clear coat to underlying primer, color coats or—worst of all—the base plastic, resin, or brass. You can color-sand lacquer single-stage colors and clear coats successfully

5 Once your sanding of the primer no longer reveals surface irregularities, apply another coat of primer and then a light coat of dark gray lacquer primer (you can tint 131 S with a few drops of flat black lacquer). You should mist on the guide coat only lightly at this stage. This is also not a bad time to drop the integrated body and floorboard onto the frame to double-check how the wheel-tire combo fits on the body. In this view, it is clear that the rear axle should be narrowed a bit to tuck the tires inside the rear fenders.

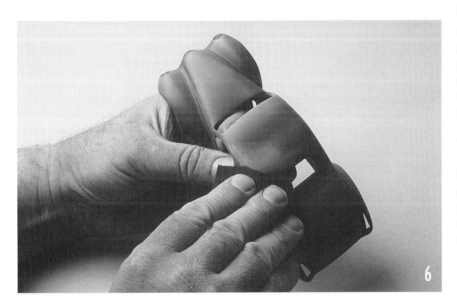

6 When the guide coat is thoroughly dry, wet-sand the body using a combination of a fine sanding stick and 600-grit sandpaper. This guide coat may reveal some very subtle surface problems, most likely scratches and minor irregularities.

7 If you cut through to the plastic or putty, lightly reprime only those areas (to avoid the unnecessary buildup of primer). Let the primer dry for a few days if you are in a dry climate, more if you are in a humid area

much sooner than enamel single-stage colors and clear coats because enamels typically take a lot longer to dry thoroughly.

Toner is a translucent element used to mix all colors, whether solids or so-called glamour or mica-pearl colors. Depending upon the ratio of the toner to the binders and other chemical agents that make up paint, the paint color might require many coats to produce the desired colors. When Joe Bailon discovered candy paint (the color red, first) in the '50s, he used various shades of red toner mixed directly in clear lacquer. Modern candy paint is a sophisticated mixture of paint elements that produces a highly translucent color. It is typically applied over a high-metallic base color (silver, bronze, or gold).

Guide coat refers to the technique of applying a very light coat of a contrasting color over the top of primer. When sanded, it reveals surface imperfections: if the guide coat is easily removed from a specific area, that place is higher than the surrounding body work. If, after a modest sanding, the material remains, in whatever shape, that area is low. Never use a regular gloss color for a guide coat. It is too dense.

Quick Tips

Never sand a color coat with any sandpaper that is coarser than 800 grit. Preferably, always use 1200 grit or finer.

Always use regular automotive sanding papers. Avoid home-improvement-store sandpapers at all costs.

Avoid using silicone-based waxes and polishes, including furniture or floor waxes, to protect your finish. They prevent continued drying of the paint job, they eventually yellow, and they prevent touchup or repainting. Use only a professional automotive polish or nonsilicone wax. Meguiar's products are recommended.

Let your paint job (whether based on hobby paints, lacquers, or urethanes) plenty of time to dry and shrink before polishing. Be patient.

Let each coat of paint "flash" before applying a new color. This is especially important for hobby enamels.

Always use eye protection and a dual-cartridge respirator when spraying paint, regardless of type.

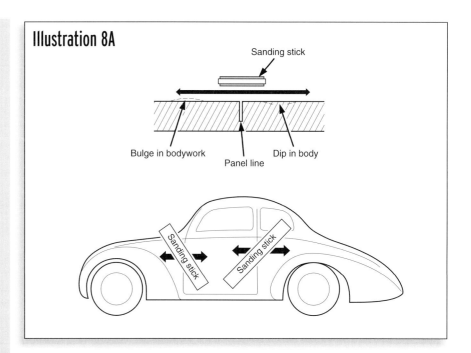

Illustration 8A

Sanding stick

Bulge in bodywork

Panel line

Dip in body

Sanding stick

Sanding stick

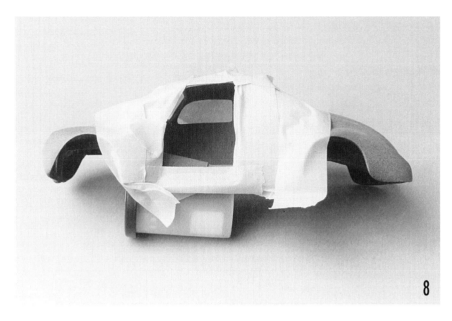

8 At this point, it is best to paint the inside of the body. Tape off the windows and mix up your chosen base color for the interior. Then airbrush the inside of the body by setting your airbrush at a medium setting. Airbrush all that you can through the door opening. Then mask over the door opening, open up the masking tape over the side windows on the other side of the body, and complete airbrushing inside the body. If you have worked carefully, there shouldn't be any interior color on the outside of the body. If there is, lightly remove it with a piece of 1200-grit sandpaper. Once the interior color has thoroughly dried, brush on 3 to 6 coats of House of Kolor Spray Mask; when the body is painted and rubbed out, simply pull up the masking material to reveal the base interior color.

9 Fashion a fixture that will fit into an area that won't receive paint. A suitable fixture can be made from an old hanger. Use two-part epoxy, mixed a bit "cool" (go light on the catalyst). Don't tape your model to the fixture—tape has a nasty habit of coming loose during painting with disastrous results.

10 Apply a medium coat of your catalyzed sealer according to the instructions: DuPont's Variprime should be mixed in a 1-to-1 mixture. Don't add any other product to the resultant mix. Apply the sealer in two coats, 5 minutes apart. Make sure that you cover all the model with the sealer. Let the sealer cure as recommended, at least 24 hours.

11 Wet-sand the entire model with 1200-grit 3M paper. Don't substitute the grits in polishing kits because those papers are ranked differently than products used by the auto industry. Wash the model with a few drops of liquid dishwashing soap, then dry.

12 Before you apply any paint, it is important to strain it. Use a standard professional autobody strainer. Mix a little thinner in the paint so that it will more quickly pass through the strainer. Use a fresh strainer every time. After an adequate amount of paint has been poured into the jar, thin it according to the formula on the chart. Right before you start to spray the paint, use a tack cloth to remove dust and other small debris. Don't wipe too hard, though, to avoid depositing the material that picks up the dust and lint on the model's surface. Discard the rag when it gets dry.

13 Our full custom 1940 Ford coupe will benefit from a coating of 1993 Jaguar color, Flamenco Pearl Metallic, overlaid with House of Kolor clear lacquer. As DuPont recommends, this color should be applied over a similarly colored base for the best effect; in this case, we will apply a quick coat of a deep metallic red base color specially mixed by Byron Bowman of Superior Paint. Apply the metallic base evenly by adjusting your airbrush to the widest setting. Spray on the color lengthwise, then at right angles to the length of the model, then at a 45 degree angle, going both ways, to avoid zebra-striping. Set the model aside to dry thoroughly. After two medium coats applied as specified, your model should look like this. Note that the paint is somewhat glossy and that the surface is relatively flat at this point.

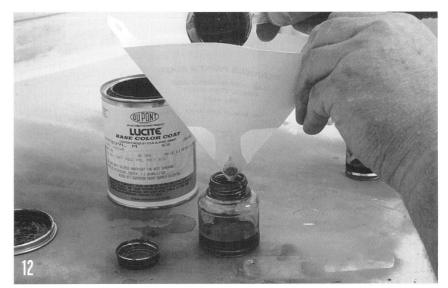

14 Once the paint has thoroughly dried for at least 24 hours (48 to 72 hours is preferable, in order to give the lacquer time to dry and shrink), it is time to apply the special 1993 Jaguar Flamenco pearl color. Strain and thin the paint as described previously, employ the paint application pattern described in the previous photo, and use a coarse nozzle with paint flow at around 35 to 40 psi. In this case, you will note that the pearl Jag color will brighten and tone the metallic red underbase, producing a kind of burnt pearl cinnamon-orange color. Remember that the more coats of this translucent mica-pearl color you apply, the richer and deeper the color will become. (Note the difference in tone between this photo and the previous one.) After the pearl color has dried for at least 72 hours, you can lay on the clear top coats. Apply three medium coats of clear and then let the model dry for one full week, more if you live in a humid or cool climate.

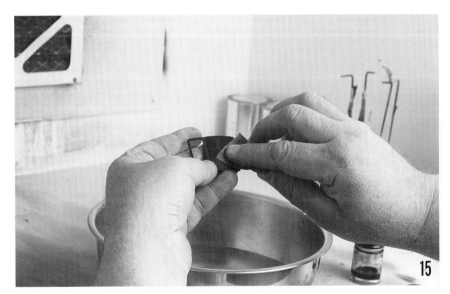

15 Once the clear coat has thoroughly dried, inspect the surface for flaws. Here comes the risky step: grab some 2000-grit 3M paper, drop a few drops of dishwashing liquid into a large bowl of warm or tepid water, and wet-sand the entire model. Don't linger in any particular spot, and stay away from ridges and other raised areas. Your goal here is to smooth the entire surface so that just a satin finish remains when you are done. Work carefully and slowly at this time. Note that we are just sanding the driver's door here; it will be attached after the interior components are installed.

16 After sanding, wash the model again in a light solution of liquid dishwashing soap, using an old soft toothbrush. Pay particular attention to panel lines and recessed areas. Remove all residue. Dry the surface with your air hose and apply two more moderate coats of clear lacquer, each thinned to 150%, waiting about 5 minutes between coats. Set the model aside to dry for at least a full day.

17 After a day, remove the fixture (it should be easier to do so if you mixed the epoxy "cool") and let the model dry for at least one week, preferably two. Halfway into the drying sequence, texture the underbody by applying a moderate "dust" coat of paint to produce a stippled appearance. Then mask the exterior painted surface with several thick, brush-applied coats of House of Kolor's Spray Mask. Here I used a mixture of very dark gray satin lacquer and Firethorn red (in a 6-to-1 ratio) on the underbody (not black because it is too jarring and obvious). After it has dried for a few hours, carefully remove the exterior masking material, including that in the headlight buckets.

18 When the model is dry, start polishing. If you were careful applying the clear coats, there should be very little dust in the lacquer. If there is a small area or two of dust, lightly sand them out with 2000-grit paper, used wet, but limit such sanding if you can. Then get a soft old diaper (the kind without the center stitching) and dampen it. Apply Meguiar's no. 3 polish to the diaper and rub the surface in a circular pattern. Support the area being polished to avoid cracking the bodywork. This will take time. You'll know you are finished when the surface is glass smooth without any texture at all. Once again, avoid ridges and other raised areas.

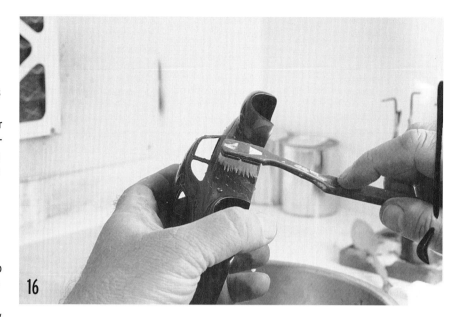

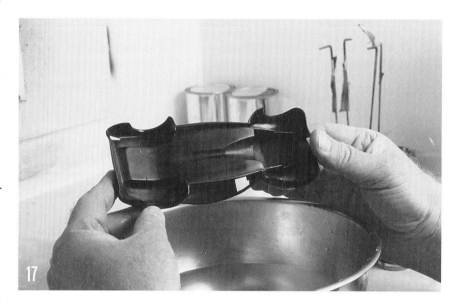

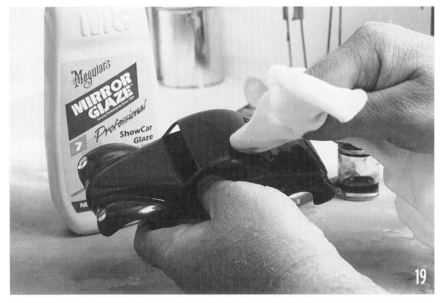

19 But there may be swirl marks that need to be removed. Wash the model gently in tepid water, dry it, and then rub the entire surface again (using another diaper) with Meguiar's M-7 as a final glaze. This product will add a luster to your hand-polished lacquer finish that will dazzle you and other hobbyists.

20 Wash the model again, clean out the residue, and dry the model. You should have a stunning, mirror-finish paint job at this stage.

21 Now it is time to assemble the interior parts (dash, door panels, carpet, seats, and so forth) and then drop the body over the finished and detailed chassis. Note that a section of the frame side rails have been spot-painted with the same color as underneath the body; now, when the body and chassis are mated, the little bit of the chassis showing beneath the body between the wheelwells will just fade away. Here, the engine-transmission and tire-wheel combinations have yet to be installed.

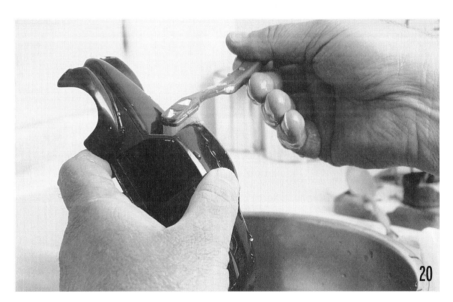

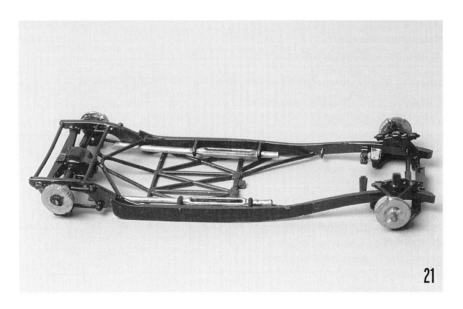

The Showroom

The models displayed here elegantly make the point that, without a doubt, the art of custom model car design and construction is the best part of the hobby.

In recent years, model car customizing has made a remarkable comeback as one of the centerpieces of the model car hobby. Leading that resurgence has been the universally respected work of some splendid scale customizers. In this gallery, let's take a close, analytical look at the work of some of the best scale model customizers today. While the models featured here do not, of course, represent all of the best scale vehicle customizing, the models here have achieved an excellent mixture of superb styling and high craftsmanship.

There are several major stylistic divisions to custom model cars, no matter when the models were constructed. The first group are the so-called "traditional" customs, which draw their inspiration from the coachbuilding designs of Sam Barris, Beldone, Bohman and Schwartz, Darrin, Derham, Fernandez, Fischer, LeBaron, Mazzara and Meyer, Pennock and Sons, Valley Custom, Westergaard, and others, all of whom were in their prime before 1958. These models feature sweeping fadeaway fenders, baroque grille work, and ground-scraping stances. They are typically painted in deep, rich colors.

The second major category of custom model cars is representative of the "show car" era from roughly 1959 through 1964. These models evoke memories of the work of the Alexander Brothers, Joe Bailon, the Barris brothers, Clarkhaiser, Herschel "Junior" Conway, Bill Cushenberrry, Bill Hines, Rod Powell, Dave Puhl, Ed Roth, Doane Spencer, Darryl Starbird of Star Customs, Neil Emory and Clayton Jensen of Valley Custom, Joe Wilhelm, Gene Winfield, and others. This era—probably the most memorable and, at times, the most excessive of all custom epochs—was short-lived but produced the greatest number of truly remarkable customs.

Finally, there are the contemporary customs, which reflect the work of modern builders whose work is animated by the history of custom car design and construction. Vehicles from the shops of Jim Bailie, Boyd Coddington, Frank DeRosa, John D'Agnostino, Larry Ericson, Greg Fluery, Sam and Chip Foose, Gary Howard, Larry Kramer, Howdy Ledbetter, Murphy and the Striper, Troy Trepanier, Elden Titus, Bill Reasoner, Mike Sydney, Jerry Sahagon, along with other builders, are widely covered in *Custom Rodder, Street Rodder, Rod & Custom,* and occasionally in *Hot Rod.* These vehicles often feature sophisticated running gear, breathtaking finishes, and the most elegant interior appointments.

Let's take a careful look at some of the best scale vehicle customs that have been constructed in the last twenty or so years. There are many more photographs of scale customs in my archives than the space here permits. I have tried to select the best examples for each of the major eras of custom car styling. The models displayed here elegantly make the point that, without a doubt, the art of custom model car design and construction is the best part of the hobby because it requires so much of each builder.

1 Dan Thomas constructed this sumptuous replica of the Hirohata Mercury, one of the first high-profile customs ever constructed. Aided by bumpers carved from aluminum, Dan's replica of a difficult subject is right on the money. Mark S. Gustavson photo

2 John White built this exquisite replica of the Barris Wildcat for the Oakland Roadster Show Diorama. The subtle paint graphics and antiseptic assembly make this model a real standout. Mark S. Gustavson photo

3 Famed diorama builder Ken Hamilton constructed this wonderfully retrograde custom based on a 1951 Chevy. He chopped the top, removed all trim, pancaked the hood and trunk, and applied beautiful candy blue finish. This is historic customizing at its best. Doug Whyte photo

4 The essence of the Matranga Mercury was perfectly captured by Bill Aitchison, one of the best and most experienced custom car builders in the hobby today. Mark S. Gustavson photo.

1

2

3

4

5 Bob Politz build this beautiful 1956 Ford with a chopped top, extended fenders, pancaked hood, and DeSoto grille. This model richly echoes the work of the Alexander Brothers in the early '60s. Rick Hanmore photo

6 Rich Tiago's Ranchero—an interesting but not beautiful car—was expertly replicated by Stan Pinnick and Jeff Morsilli for the Oakland Roadster Show Diorama project. Mark S. Gustavson photo

7 Another replica—this time of Pat Mulligan's '58 Chevy—was expertly crafted by AMB member Frank Olsen. This model required a lot of work—it was sectioned and chopped and received 1961 Oldsmobile rear quarter panels. Mark S. Gustavson photo

8 Bob Barnett also constructed this striking replica of Dave Bugarin's Mercury. Bob's passion led him to replicate the colors precisely by using original lacquer toners for the paint. Mark S. Gustavson photo

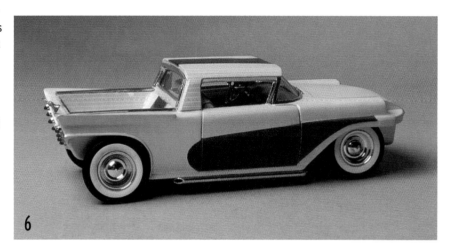

9 I built this 1951 Mercury convertible—complete with a Carson-styled removable top, and built from a 1949 Mercury—in 1980. I extended the rear fenders vertically, drew the side character line in a straight line to frame the rear fender skirts, frenched the headlights, and flipped and installed 1956 Ford bumpers. Mark S. Gustavson photo

9

10

12

10 Victor Collins, a noted replica custom builder, constructed this replica of an early Sam Barris custom 1952 Ford convertible. The duplication of the original side trim, grille work, and interior appointments is impressive. Rick Hanmore photo

11 David Dale crafted this sleek, beautiful '49 Mercury. A gracefully chopped top, nicely resolving itself into the tulip panel and trunk, highlight this swoop custom. David Dale photo

12 Another interesting aspect of custom model car building is replicating old box art models. Rick Hanmore built this spot-on reproduction of the cover custom car art on AMT's 1961 customizing kits. Rick Hanmore photo

13 Though overstyled in some ways, my Mercari is the favorite model I have completed to date. The body is a combination of brass and plastic, with opening panels, operating lights, and dozens of photoetched parts specially created by Bob Wick. This model won Best Auto at the 1995 IPMS Nationals. Jan Stevenson photo

14 This beautiful 1957 Ford by Jack Pennington was sectioned, chopped, and treated to a lovely dip as the rear fenders meet the door. It features more subtle customizing tricks than can be listed here. Jack Pennington photo

15 Tim Boyd's Tangerine Dream is an excellent example of a mild custom. The lengthened rear fenders nicely balance the hardtop styling. The horizontal stripes really add to the sleekness that Tim successfully captured. An added element of this model is the exquisite detailing. Tim Boyd photo

16 I built this full custom 1972 Corvette, which features extended fenders, a widened body, a 1964 Corvette roof, and three murals and other graphic paintwork. The suspension and the steering also operate. Mark S. Gustavson photo

13

14

15

16

the show car era

17 Even vehicles intended for competition can have custom body work. This highly modified Beetle, built by competition modeler Don Fahrni, was chopped, channeled, molded, and treated to a quarter-window filling operation. Doug Whyte photo

18 Andy "Moose" Kallen built this 1951 Chevy, roughly patterned after the famed Goulart Oldsmobile. Andy's work is always first-rate. Mark S. Gustavson photo

19 One of the most innovative customizers these days is Joel Dirnberger. His Shark mates a highly modified 1963 Corvette roadster body to a '30s Chevy frame and engine. However unpredictably, the design works and, of course, Joel's work is first-rate. Joel Dirnberger photo

20 This subtle RX-7 was built by master machinist Cody Grayland. The least obvious feature is that he extended the rocker panels downward two scale inches—an interesting reversal of sectioning—in order to introduce better balance to the body. Revised front end styling, flared wheel wells, and a smoothed body, topped with a tuxedo black finish, demonstrate that modern customs can be any subject. Mark S. Gustavson photo

20

the contemporary era

21 Ray Patrick's radical and beautiful 1959 Chevy features a 1961 Chevy roof expertly integrated into the body. This car combines many traditional customizing motifs (shortened side trim, rolled pans) with modern running gear and contemporary interior appointments. Doug Whyte photo

22 This 1961 Mercury recently came from my workbench. I fitted a '61 Starliner roof, moved the door rearward on the body, and lengthened it (thereby lengthening the front fenders). I removed all side trim and opened up the rear wheel wells to match the front. The lengthwise hood and trunk lines, which were straightened, now parallel the body. I retained the stock front and rear grille work and bumpers; Lincoln-Mercury could have built this styling study in the early '60s. Mark S. Gustavson photo

23 Gary Grassman turned a Viper into this very interesting experimental concept roadster, one-upping the Prowler! Custom model building can produce interesting styling studies like this one, which appeared at the GSL Reunion. Photo by *Scale Auto Enthusiast* staff

21

22

23

24 This beautiful 1951 Chevy was constructed by Vince LoBosco. He reworked the roof line and glass, opened all the panels, and fitted modern running gear and interior appointments to the model. Rick Hanmore photo

24

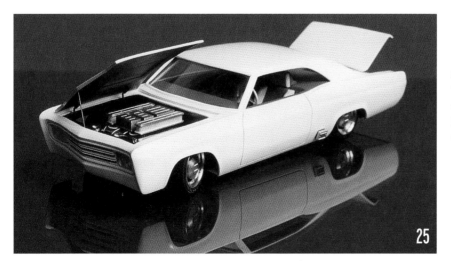

25 Pat Covert produced this innovative custom, called Future Shock, which mates smoothed bodywork, revised front and rear-end treatments, contemporary running gear, and a monochomatic paint job. Pat Covert photo

25

the contemporary era

26

26 I built this sectioned, chopped and narrowed '49 Mercury. It was dropped over a modified unibody frame to which I fitted a '67 Eldorado front drive. I straightened out the traditional character line down the side and rolled it around the back edge of the body, terminating it just about at each headlight. The model features opened-up wheel wells for a more sporty look and a reshaped top to echo the '61 Ford Starliner roof. Mark S. Gustavson photo

27 One of the more stunning scale customs in recent years is this 1951 Studebaker by Doug Whyte. He extended the rear fenders, designed a new greenhouse, extended the lower front grille and enlarged the wheel wells. The high-tech drive train completes this beautiful model, which is topped with a stunning pearl white paint job. Doug Whyte photo

27

28 Our project model is an interesting interpretation of an age-old subject. The decision to wedge-shape the body and dramatically reduce the frontal aspect, adds a modern touch to a vintage body. The comparison with my mild custom, built in a vintage style, emphasizes the significant styling changes brought about by chopping the top, sectioning the body, and molding everything together in a seamless whole. Mark S. Gustavson photo

28

29 This gracefully restyled 1965 Chevy Impala was designed and built by Bill Taylor. He dropped the body over the frame, grafted the first and last five scale inches of a '69 Chevelle to the '65 Chevy body, and widened the rear window for a more airy appearance The coke-bottle flow of the rear fenders is a beautiful shape, and Bill has achieved a lithe form by opening up the rear wheel wells. Mark S. Gustavson photo

the contemporary era

30 Larry Booth built this sectioned 1949 Ford, which features a chopped top with a rear window that was laid forward, slanted B pillars, pancaked hood and trunk, and some design elements from the 1990 T-Bird Super Coupe, along with the Super Coupe drive train. This is a good example of a traditional custom subject mated with contemporary engine and suspension components. Jan Stevenson photo

31 A new face in the scale customizing scene is Tim Kolankiewicz, who built his Coral Aura based on a 1961 Chevy. Tim chopped the roof, laid back the windshield, shortened up the side trim, and emphasized the lowness of the model with a two-tone paint job. The outsized wheel and tire combo adds to the aggressive appearance of this risk-taking modern custom. Rick Hanmore photo

32 From the rear—possibly the best aspect of this model—our custom '40 Ford takes on a decidedly modern appearance. The long taillights pick up the sweep of the rear fenders and the creation of new window shapes in the chopped top (which sweeps into the tulip panel) neatly sidesteps the usual custom '40 Ford. Even though the body has been substantially channeled over the new frame, adequate ground clearance is maintained so that this vehicle could be driven. Mark S. Gustavson photo

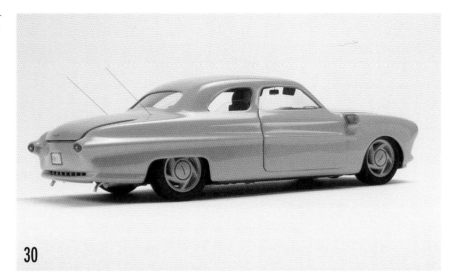

30

31

32